THE
7 PLACES
Jesus
SHED HIS
BLOOD

THE
7 PLACES
Jesus
SHED HIS
BLOOD

WHITAKER
HOUSE

This text has been excerpted from *Free at Last: Removing the Past from Your Future*, © 2000, 2004 by Larry Huch, pp. 95–174. Excerpted with permission of the publisher, Whitaker House (www.whitakerhouse.com). All rights reserved.

The 7 Places Jesus Shed His Blood

Larry Huch Ministries
P.O. Box 610890
Dallas, TX 75261
972.313.7133
www.newbeginnings.org / www.LarryHuchMinistries.com

ISBN: 978-1-60374-246-7
Printed in the United States of America
© 2000, 2004 by Larry Huch

Whitaker House
1030 Hunt Valley Circle
New Kensington, PA 15068
www.whitakerhouse.com

Library of Congress Cataloging-in-Publication Data

Huch, Larry.
  [Free at last. Selections]
  The 7 places Jesus shed his blood / by Larry Huch.
    p. cm.
  ISBN 978-1-60374-246-7 (trade pbk. : alk. paper) 1. Families—Religious
  life. 2. Blessing and cursing. 3. Jesus Christ—Blood. I. Title.
  BV4526.3.H83 2012
  248.8'6—dc23
                        2011051075

1 2 3 4 5 6 7 8 9 10   **W**   18 17 16 15 14 13 12

CONTENTS

CHAPTER 1

THE BLOOD OF JESUS HAS MORE POWER THAN YOU KNOW

Week after week, we receive letters from believers expressing a need to be set free. We also receive many letters from people who are not born-again Christians but who are desperate for answers to their problems. There are people all over this nation who battle generational curses on their own life or on their family's lives—depression, suicide, illnesses of all kinds, uncontrolled lust, promiscuity, anxiety, failure, poverty, abandonment, witchcraft, fear, rebellion, abuse, and addictions of every kind. The list goes on.

One letter came from a man who said that he wept uncontrollably as he listened to my testimony. He told us that my story could have been his story, except that he had already lost his wife and kids because of his raging, out-of-control anger. He had become hopeless as he tried everything he could think of to change his life. He failed every time. He even said he would rather be the victim, the person who was abused, than be the abuser, because as an abuser he had to live with the horrible shame and guilt.

There is a lot of attention focused on the victims of abuse, and rightly so, but this man pleaded, "I'm an abuser, but I'm a victim too, a victim of my own rage. Please help me to change." My heart broke as memories and feelings from my past flooded over me. I saw how desperately people need to know how they can be set free.

When I hear these stories and read these letters, I weep before God. I am reminded of what Hosea the prophet said: "*My people are destroyed for lack of knowledge*" (Hosea 4:6). As a result, I am determined to get the Word of God to those who are being trampled underfoot by Satan, to those who are worn-out and ready to give up in defeat. The enemy does not spare any tactics in trying to defeat God's people. Nothing is beyond demonic assault. Nothing, that is, except the blood of Jesus.

THE POWER OF THE BLOOD

The blood of Jesus is the power source for our salvation and our freedom. The moment we receive Jesus Christ into our hearts and lives, we are forgiven for our sins. Jesus then becomes *Jehovah-Tsidkenu*, our righteousness, and *Jehovah-M'kaddesh*, our ongoing sanctification.

We are made righteous by the blood of Jesus that washes away every sin we ever committed. That means we are no longer enemies of God; instead, we are in right relationship with Him. The blood of Jesus does not simply cover up our sin. The good news of Jesus Christ is far better than that! I don't care if the sin is drug addiction, abortion, lying, or stealing;

when we claim the blood of Jesus, His blood washes that sin away.

> *Though your sins are like scarlet, they shall be as white as snow; though they are red like crimson, they shall be as wool.*
> (Isaiah 1:18)

Our sins are like a deep-dyed stain that can't come out in a normal washing. But though our sins are deep-dyed stains, the blood of Jesus makes us whiter than snow. From God's perspective, the blood of Jesus cleanses us so we appear before Him as if we had never sinned. (See Acts 3:19.)

As good as that is—and that news is great because it is the hope for our lives—it is not the whole story of our salvation. What many Christians do not know is that their salvation is not limited to forgiveness of sins. The God who said to me many years ago, "Larry, your sins are forgiven," is the same God who said, "Cocaine, be gone. Alcohol, be gone. Poverty, be gone. Disease, anger, and violence, be gone." *He is the same God!*

God's plan for our lives is not turmoil, strife, and pain. His plan for our lives is joy, peace, and happiness. Today in my personal life, my marriage, and my family, I am living dreams I never thought possible. I couldn't stop doing drugs by my own determination or by the strength of my own willpower, but Jesus delivered me. Methadone couldn't cure me. Acupuncture couldn't cure me. Hypnosis couldn't cure me. But the blood of Jesus did the work, and it was a complete work!

MORE THAN CONQUERORS

As Christians, we are grateful that God redeemed us, washing away the sin and destruction in our lives. But our salvation involves more than forgiveness of sins.

If you confess with your mouth the Lord Jesus and believe in your heart that God has raised Him from the dead, you will be saved. (Romans 10:9)

I believe this is the greatest promise in the Bible. The word "*saved*" in the Greek language, in which the New Testament was originally written, is the word *sozo*. It means to be completely whole. When Jesus talked about our being saved, He was not just talking about being forgiven and becoming a Christian. Salvation means receiving everything that is ours—everything that was paid for by the blood of Jesus. That means we are forgiven, but it also means we are healed, delivered, prosperous, blessed, and set free. The salvation Jesus Christ has for us is *forgiveness, healing, deliverance, prosperity, freedom, authority,* and *power.*[1]

Romans 8:37 says, "*We are more than conquerors through Him who loved us.*" When we realistically assess everything we are facing, take stock of our own resources (our own strength and power and our own ability to work things out), and see that the odds are stacked against us, then we need to turn to God and find out what He has for us. We need to know the truth that will set us free. And the truth is that, by the power of the shed blood of Jesus Christ, we are not going under—we are going over. No matter how big the giant is that we are facing, in Jesus Christ we are more than conquerors.

When all the circumstances of your life spell defeat, when it seems like people want to keep you down, when everything says you are going to lose, remember, *you are not going to lose because you were born to win*. You are going to win if you don't faint, if you take a stand, and if you rise up like a warrior and say, "In the name of Jesus Christ and in the power of His blood, I am not going under; I am going over. Victory is mine!"

It doesn't matter what you are facing—marriage problems, health problems, financial problems, spiritual problems, alcohol, drugs, cigarettes—Jesus is right here and is your salvation, your redemption, and your deliverance right now. Your *sozo*—your salvation, healing, and deliverance—is here, not in the sweet by and by, but *right now*. I like to say it this way: Not in the sweet by-and-by when I die, but down on the ground while I'm still around!

The enemy never gives up. He never rests in his battle to defeat us. When we are made righteous by the blood of Jesus, we haven't fought the last battle, but we are now on the winning side. The enemy will continue his assaults, attempting to capture our minds and control our emotions, but we can defeat the enemy and live in victory every day.

The devil comes to you and says, "You know what? You still have that anger problem. You'll never change. You still have that depression problem. You'll never change. You still have that alcohol or drug problem. You'll never change." Your accuser says, "You've been born again, but you're a hypocrite because you are going through your second divorce, and you will never change." You are standing before the throne of grace, but the devil is still accusing you day and night. The Father leans down and asks, "How do you plead?" You know the accusations are true because you really have these faults.

You look up at the Father and say, "Guilty." Then the Father leans down and says, "Don't plead guilty, son. Don't plead guilty, daughter. Plead the blood of Jesus. Don't plead alcohol; plead the blood. Don't plead failure; plead the blood. Don't plead poverty; plead the blood. You have been redeemed by the blood of Jesus."

Experts and streetwise friends told my mom and dad, "Your son will never change." And I could not change on my own. I was born again and couldn't change. I was Spirit-filled, and I couldn't change. Then I found out about the power of the blood of Jesus for my life, and I stood up and said, "Devil, you are already defeated. I am set free by the blood of Jesus." When Jesus hung on the cross, He said, "*It is finished!*" (John 19:30). The blood covenant between God and man has been completed. Everything you need has been paid in full by the blood of Jesus.

People used to tell me, "You'll never change. You will never be free." The world says, "Once a junkie, always a junkie." That may be what the world says, but the Word says something else: "*If the Son makes you free, you shall be free indeed*" (John 8:36).

We can tell the kids in our schools, "You know what? When you say no to drugs, there is a power that will give you strength on the inside. You don't have to be drawn back into drugs and alcohol."

We can go into our prisons with the message of hope and overcoming. One of our prison ministries at New Beginnings Christian Center had to go to double services because of the revival that occurred. One of the inmates with whom we minister in the prison is a "lifer" and is helping to lead one of our Bible studies. He was brought before the members of the state legislature, who said to him, "Eighty-two percent of the convicts return to prison on another conviction after being released from a previous sentence. Now after six years, only two guys from your group have gone back to prison. The rest of them are out working at their jobs and supporting their families. What's the difference? Tell us why that happens."

He told the legislators, "Number one, Jesus Christ has taken the burden of our sin, and He has washed us clean. He's given us a new beginning. We are born again, and we are here to tell you that He's not only the burden-remover, but He is also the yoke-destroyer. We don't have to go back to jail. We don't have to rob again. We don't have to steal again. We don't have to batter our wives anymore. We don't have to do dope anymore. We don't have to have alcohol anymore. Jesus is alive in us. He rose again. He paid the price for us."

These inmates are being set free and are staying free by the blood of Jesus Christ.

The Jewish people understood the teaching of the blood. When they needed forgiveness, they put blood on the altar of the temple. When they needed mercy, they put blood on the mercy seat. When they needed to hear from God, they put blood on the veil so they could enter into the Holy of Holies and be in the presence of God. When they needed peace, they

brought a blood sacrifice. When they needed healing, they brought a blood sacrifice. Every time they
needed a miracle, they offered a blood sacrifice. (See
Leviticus 1–7.)

For you and me, there is a river that never runs
dry. It is the source of all God wants to do in our
lives and through our lives. It is the ongoing river of
the blood of Jesus. Under the new covenant, we don't
have to apply it every single time we need a miracle,
every time we need to enter into God's presence, and
every time we need healing. All we have to do is realize that the powerful blood of Jesus Christ is there
for us to call upon any and every time we need a
touch from God.

LAW OR GRACE?

After Jesus ascended and returned to heaven,
there was a debate by His followers about whether we
are saved by obeying the requirements of the law or
by accepting the grace of Jesus Christ.

> *For as many as are of the works of the
> law are under the curse; for it is written,
> "Cursed is everyone who does not continue
> in all things which are written in the book
> of the law, to do them." But that no one is
> justified by the law in the sight of God is
> evident, for "the just shall live by faith." Yet
> the law is not of faith, but "the man who
> does them shall live by them." Christ has
> redeemed us from the curse of the law, hav-
> ing become a curse for us (for it is written,
> "Cursed is everyone who hangs on a tree"),*

that the blessing of Abraham might come upon the Gentiles in Christ Jesus, that we might receive the promise of the Spirit through faith. (Galatians 3:10–14)

The person who believes he is saved by his own righteousness has to be perfectly righteous in every single matter. If a person thinks he is saved by following the rules and requirements of the law, then he is going to have to follow the law in everything he does or the curse of the law will come upon him.

People often say we are redeemed from the law, therefore we are free from moral obligations or requirements. But what Galatians 3:13 says is that we are redeemed from the *curse* of the law because Christ Jesus became the curse for us. Every sin that anyone ever committed has a curse on it. Jesus not only took our sins on Himself, but He also took our curse for the sin. *Jesus has redeemed us from the curse of our sin.*

Our finances, marriages, homes, emotions, and minds have been kidnapped by the devil. But Jesus came and paid the ransom for every area of our lives in full and has brought us back to the way we are supposed to be.

I have set before you life and death, blessing and cursing; therefore choose life, that both you and your descendants may live.
(Deuteronomy 30:19)

The law of Moses contained both a blessing and a curse. If you followed the commandments of God, doing everything that God says, then there would be blessings on you, your family, your city, and your nation. If you didn't honor God or follow His instructions, then a curse would come on you, your family, your city, your state, and your nation. If you did what was right, you would be blessed. If you did what was wrong, then a curse would come upon you.

But believers in Jesus Christ aren't bound by the law of Moses. By Jesus' death on the cross, Jesus became the curse so that we can be delivered from the curse and be a blessing to our family, church, city, and nation. Poverty is a curse. Sickness is a curse. Disease is a curse. Divorce is a curse. Drugs, alcohol, and abuse are all part of the curse. When we are under the blood of Jesus, we are redeemed from the curse. As He hung dying on the cross, Jesus said, "*It is finished!*" (John 19:30). Our redemption through the new blood covenant was made complete at the cross.

> *Knowing that you were not redeemed with corruptible things, like silver or gold, from your aimless conduct received by tradition from your fathers, but with the precious blood of Christ, as of a lamb without blemish and without spot.* (1 Peter 1:18–19)

Our redemption is total, and it covers everything that Jesus shed His blood for, which is every part of us and every one of us. The only way redemption can fall short is if we don't know it and don't apply it. The devil does not want you to get knowledge of the blood of the Lamb, because if you do not have knowledge of the overcoming power of the blood, then the devil can overcome you. However, by gaining that knowledge and applying it to your life, you can overcome the devil.

There is nothing defeated about Christianity. There is nothing unvictorious in Christianity. When Jesus hung on the cross, instead of defeat, He shouted with the voice of victory, "*It is finished!*" (John 19:30).

For the message of the cross is foolishness to those who are perishing, but to us who are being saved it is the power of God.
(1 Corinthians 1:18)

Christianity is not a weak religion. It's not a just-get-by religion, or a run-and-hide religion. Christianity is a strong religion because greater is He who is in us than he who is in the world. (See 1 John 4:4.) Our accuser, Satan, has been cast down and defeated by the shed blood of Jesus Christ.

Then I heard a loud voice saying in heaven, "Now salvation, and strength, and the kingdom of our God, and the power of His Christ have come, for the accuser of our brethren, who accused them before our God day and night, has been cast down. And they overcame him by the blood of the Lamb and by the word of their testimony, and they did not love their lives to the death."
(Revelation 12:10–11)

The way we overcome the enemy is by the blood of the Lamb. We are not going to overcome the devil through methadone. We are not going to overcome the devil through hypnosis. We are not going to overcome the devil by a year or even a lifetime of professional counseling. The word "*overcame*" in the above passage does not mean they "got by." It does not mean they escaped. It does not mean they hid. You can't say, "I'll just hide from the devil." The devil knows where you live. He's got your house number, phone number, Social Security number, credit card number, and bank account number!

The word "*overcame*" in Revelation 12:11 means "conquered," "prevailed," and "got the victory."[2] I have realized through the Word of God that it is not by my own might, by my own rights, because I pray and fast, or don't smoke, cuss, chew, or go out with those who do, that I can overcome. No, we overcome by the blood of the Lamb.

Not only is the devil *not* going to get me, but *I* am going to get *him*! We are not called to stay in the land we are in now—we are called to take the Promised Land. We can take the streets. We can take back our schools. We can take our judicial system. We can take back the government through the blood of Jesus. We are told to overcome, not to be neutral and not to do okay. We can do better than okay. We can overcome through the blood of Jesus!

We received this letter from a man who recently experienced the fullness of his blood-bought salvation.

> *Dear Pastor Larry Huch,*
>
> *I thank God for your anointing to bring deliverance to God's children. I've been saved and filled with the Holy Spirit since 1983, but I still carried addictions, anger, and deep hurts. God is still at work in my life "cleaning up my mess," so to speak.*
>
> *Recently, I listened to a cassette tape series of your message "Breaking Family Curses." I felt*

burdened greatly as I jotted down notes and listened to every word. I got to the last tape of the set and you prayed and bound the powers of darkness, but I didn't think or feel I was delivered.

I stopped the last tape, and as I walked toward my bedroom door, "Pow!" It hit me like a great rainstorm from heaven. I felt God's hand and the power of the Holy Spirit engulf me. I tried to remain standing, but I could not. I dropped to my hands and knees, but my arms could not support me. I yielded to this power and lay prostrate on the floor. I tried to get back up, but the power and electricity going through me kept me on the floor. When I did get back up, I felt totally different—I felt free for the first time in my Christian life! Since that day I have not had to struggle as in the past but am walking in total victory and freedom!

I thank God for ministers like you who not only speak about God, but have experiences such as you have had. This gives you a hands-on ability to know that what God did for you, He can do for others like me.

Grateful and blessed through you,

Jay

There is power in the blood of the Lamb. It is available to me, and it is available to you. You can be free in every part of your life and in everything that concerns you because of the blood of Jesus.

For those wishing to review the points highlighted in this book, a series of discussion questions may be found at the end of each chapter.

DISCUSSION QUESTIONS

1. Read Hosea 4:6. What does the prophet Hosea say about why people are destroyed?

   From lack of Knowledge + rejection of Knowledge

2. What does Isaiah 1:18 say about our sins?

   They are as scarlet + crimson, but the blood of Jesus makes us white as snow

3. From God's perspective, what does the blood of Jesus do to our sin? See Acts 3:19.

   Wipes them out

4. Read Romans 10:9 to discover the greatest promise in the Bible. Write it here: *If you declare with your mouth Jesus is Lord + believe in your heart that God raised Him from the dead, you will be saved.*

5. According to Romans 8:37, we are more than *Conquerors* through Him who loved us.

   Nothing will separate us from the love of God.

6. After Jesus ascended and returned to heaven, there was a debate by His followers about whether we are saved by obeying the requirements of the law or by accepting the grace of Jesus Christ. After reading Galatians 3:10–14, write down your thoughts concerning this matter.

   Jesus redeeded us from the curse of sin so that through Him and by faith we receive the promise of eternal life.

7. Read Deuteronomy 30:19 and fill in the blanks below.

I have set before you __life__ *and* __death__ *, blessing and cursing; therefore choose* __life__ *, that both you and your descendants may live.*

8. When Jesus hung on the cross, what did He shout in victory? Read John 19:30.

It is finished!

9. What is the message of the cross to those who are saved? See 1 Corinthians 1:18.

It is the power of God.

10. According to 1 John 4:4, how are Christians reassured of God's greatness and His ability to win in our lives? He is greater than the one who is in the world

11. Read Revelation 12:10–11 and answer the following questions:

(a) What has become of our accuser, the devil?

He has been hurled down

(b) How do believers overcome the devil and his plans?

By the blood of the lamb and the word of their testimony.

CHAPTER 2

IN GETHSEMANE, JESUS WON BACK OUR WILLPOWER

Knowing that you were not redeemed
with perishable things like silver or gold
from your futile way of life inherited from
your forefathers, but with precious blood,
as of a lamb unblemished and spotless,
the blood of Christ.
—1 Peter 1:18–19 NASB

In the Lord's Prayer, Jesus taught us how to pray. I believe we can identify seven places of power in the Lord's Prayer. Furthermore, in the Old Testament tabernacle, which housed the presence of God, there were seven places of power and anointing. Now we are the new tabernacle of God. We house the presence of God with a new covenant—a seven-fold blood covenant.

In the sixteenth chapter of Leviticus, we read that the people brought two goats to the tabernacle. One goat was for the atonement of sin. The second goat was to have the blood of the first goat placed on its head and then be released into the desert.

Before the mercy seat he shall sprinkle some of the blood with his finger seven times…. Then he shall sprinkle some of the blood on it with his finger seven times, cleanse it, and consecrate it. (Leviticus 16:14, 19)

At two different times, the high priest would sprinkle the blood with his finger seven times. When I preach this, I'll often ask, "How many know that we're redeemed by the blood?" Everyone answers yes. Then I'll ask, "Do you know where the blood was shed?" And everyone always says, "At the cross." That's true; Jesus' blood was shed at the cross. However, His blood was not shed just one time, but seven different times. The source of the power of God for every area of our lives is in the shed blood of Jesus Christ. Jesus shed His blood in seven places that you and I might be made whole, forgiven of our sins, and set free from the bondage of sin and the iniquity that has entered into our families.

The power of Christ's blood flows from His complete work in giving His life and rising again, but we can look at the individual stages to glean insight into what His sacrifice gives us.

The first place Jesus shed His blood was in the Garden of Gethsemane on the night of the Last Supper with His disciples. It's not a coincidence that the first place Jesus ransomed us or shed His redemptive blood was in a garden, because the first place we lost the power of God's blessing was in another garden, the Garden of Eden.

The word *redeemed* means that we are ransomed or brought back to the original place.[3] That original place with the original blessing is everything we had in the Garden of Eden.

I've heard people say, "I have no willpower. I want to stop overeating, smoking, losing my temper (or whatever is out of control in their lives), but I have no willpower." We lost our willpower to do what is right, to do what is best for us, to do what is healthy, and to do what will bring benefit and blessing when Adam disobeyed God in the Garden of Eden. Eve was deceived by the serpent, but Adam willfully disobeyed God. In other words, Eve was deceived by Satan, but Adam made a choice to disobey God.

God had told Adam, "All in the garden is yours except the Tree of the Knowledge of Good and Evil." (See Genesis 3:17.) In essence, Adam said, "Father, not Your will, but mine be done," and at that moment, Adam sacrificed man's willpower in every area. With Adam's disobedience, we gave our will over to the enemy and lost our ability to say yes to all the good God has for us and no to all the bad the enemy wants to do to us. The willpower we lost in the Garden of Eden was won back in the Garden of Gethsemane when Jesus said, "Not My will, but Thy will be done." (See Matthew 26:39.)

JESUS MADE THE CHOICE— KNOWING EVERYTHING

Jesus was both God and man. Being God, He knew what His accusers were going to do to Him. He knew they were going to rip the beard from His face. He knew they were going to take Him to the whipping post and beat Him until the organs of His body showed out His back. He knew they were going to strip Him, hang Him naked, and spit on Him. He knew they were going to put that tree on His back.

He knew they were going to take the crown of thorns and jam those three-and-a-half-inch thorns down into His skull. He knew they were going to take those spikes and pound them into His hands and into His feet. He knew they were going to take that spear and jam it into His side. He was God, and He knew what was about to happen to Him.

Being man, He knew He was going to feel the whip on His back. He knew He would feel the beard being pulled from His face. He knew He would feel the nails being pounded into His hands. He would not escape the pain and the humiliation. In the Garden of Gethsemane, Jesus knew what was going to happen to Him. His spirit was willing to do what God wanted Him to do, but His flesh was weak and wanted to escape the agony and the torture He was about to endure. Jesus faced the same battle that Adam faced—whether to follow His will or the will of the Father.

> *O My Father, if it is possible, let this cup pass from Me; nevertheless, not as I will, but as You will.*   (Matthew 26:39)

The Bible says Jesus got up from praying, went to speak to His disciples, came back to His place of prayer, and prayed the same prayer a second and a third time. (See Matthew 26:40–44.) There was a struggle going on inside Jesus—the will of the Father versus the will of the man.

> *Then an angel appeared to Him from heaven, strengthening Him. And being in agony,*

He prayed more earnestly. Then His sweat became like great drops of blood falling down to the ground. When He rose up from prayer, and had come to His disciples, He found them sleeping from sorrow. Then He said to them, "Why do you sleep? Rise and pray, lest you enter into temptation."

(Luke 22:43–46)

This is how Jesus shed His blood in the Garden. Medical doctors confirm that at times of intense fear or agony, a person's blood vessels can literally break beneath the skin, and blood will begin to come out of his pores like sweat. Out of Jesus' pores came sweat and blood because of the anxiety, the fear, and the turmoil He was experiencing. Why is this significant? We must keep in mind that we've been redeemed by the blood. The first Adam surrendered our willpower to Satan. The second Adam, Jesus, redeemed our willpower by saying, "Father, not My will, but Thy will," and sweating great drops of blood. This is where we gain back our willpower to overcome the drug problems, the alcohol problems, the anger problems, and the depression problems.

Jesus knew what was going to happen to Him. His spirit and His flesh were battling, but He won the victory when He submitted to the will of the Father. Jesus won the battle, broke the curse, redeemed us, and gave us back our willpower.

WILLPOWER RESTORED

When the devil comes against us to say, "You cannot change. You're not strong enough," we have the willpower to rise in victory because Jesus said,

"Not My will, but Thine be done." Because Jesus shed His blood in the Garden of Gethsemane, you can say yes to the will of God for your life and no to the enemy of your life.

Before I knew the Lord, I was desperate to quit drugs. I would take that needle, stick it in my arm, get high, and throw up. Then I would say, "I'm not going to do this anymore. I am going to quit now and quit forever." I would stand on the front porch of my cabin out in the woods where I lived and throw that needle as far as I could possibly throw it. But within two hours, I would be out in the woods, crawling on my hands and knees, going through the leaves and brush trying to find that needle so I could mainline again.

I couldn't quit.

I used to be full of hate, violence, and anger, and I would say, "I don't want to explode in this anger anymore. I don't want to be like this anymore." I tried to quit. I wanted to, but I couldn't. I had no willpower. My spirit was willing, but my flesh was weak. (See Matthew 26:41.)

How is it that Jesus can set us free when we cannot do it on our own? Because when Jesus sweat drops of blood in the Garden of Gethsemane, our willpower was redeemed and given back to us. What Adam lost in the Garden of Eden was restored in the Garden of Gethsemane. All we have to do is say, "I plead the blood of Jesus."

SURRENDER CONTROL

But Moses said to God, "Who am I, that I should go to Pharaoh and bring the Israelites out of Egypt?" And God said, "I will be with you. And this will be the sign to you that it is I who have sent you: When you have brought the people out of Egypt, you will worship God on this mountain." Moses said to God, "Suppose I go to the Israelites and say to them, 'The God of your fathers has sent me to you,' and they ask me, 'What is his name?' Then what shall I tell them?" God said to Moses, "I Am Who I Am. This is what you are to say to the Israelites: 'I Am has sent me to you.'" God also said to Moses, "Say to the Israelites, 'The Lord, the God of your fathers—the God of Abraham, the God of Isaac and the God of Jacob—has sent me to you.' This is my name forever, the name by which I am to be remembered from generation to generation."

(Exodus 3:11–15 NIV)

"*I Am*" in these verses is translated from *Yahweh* and can be translated, "I will be everything you need Me to be whenever you need Me to be it."[4] God told Moses, "Tell My children I Am has sent you. I will be their everything." He is the same I Am for us today as He was for the children of Israel. God delivered the Israelites from bondage and captivity, and He is waiting to deliver you from whatever bondage you are in through the power of the blood of Jesus Christ.

Jesus therefore, knowing all things that should come upon him, went forth, and said unto them, Whom seek ye? They answered him, Jesus of Nazareth. Jesus saith unto them, I am he. And Judas also, which

*betrayed him, stood with them. As soon
then as he had said unto them, I am he,
they went backward, and fell to the ground.
Then asked he them again, Whom seek ye?
And they said, Jesus of Nazareth. Jesus
answered, I have told you that I am he: if
therefore ye seek me, let these go their way.*
(John 18:4–8 KJV)

— The King James Version italicizes the word
"*he*," which means we put it there. When they asked
for Jesus of Nazareth, He really responded, "I AM."
Immediately they fell to the ground because of the
anointing of God. Jesus is I AM for us today. He is the
source for everything we need. If you need strength,
Jesus is your strength. If you need wisdom, Jesus is
your wisdom. If you are ready to submit your will to
Him, He is there to give you the power to do that. You
can choose to do the will of God.

Until I gave God control of my desires and surrendered my will to Him, I was out of control. Even
as a Christian, I was out of control until I yielded
complete control to Him and allowed Him to direct
my desires and change my will. I had to resist the
devil. I said, "I am *not* going to let this anger control
me. I am *not* going to let these things control me. I
am *not*." I had to yield control of my will to God's will.
I prayed, "Father, I give You my will. I submit to the
great I AM." When I did that, Jesus Christ strength-
ened my will to do His will.

Each of us has to make up our own mind and
choose God's will or our will. We can pray the prayer
of Jesus by the power of the blood of Jesus: "Father,
not my will, but Thine be done."

KNOWING WHO YOU ARE

*For if anyone is a hearer of the word and not
a doer, he is like a man observing his natural face in a mirror; for he observes himself,
goes away, and immediately forgets what
kind of man he was. But he who looks into
the perfect law of liberty and continues in
it, and is not a forgetful hearer but a doer of
the work, this one will be blessed in what
he does.* (James 1:23–25)

This passage of Scripture says that we go to the
mirror (the Word of God) and see what the Bible says
we are, but when we walk away, we forget who we are
in Jesus. I heard a man preaching on this one time,
and his theory was that the Word of God reminds us
how sinful and worthless we are, but as soon as we
walk away, we forget all about it. Now, that may be
one way of looking at it, but I believe God is showing
us something completely different.

The devil doesn't want us to experience all the
power and blessings that are ours through Jesus
Christ, so he does everything he can to make us
feel like we'll never win or accomplish anything. The
Word of God is like a mirror. When we look in it, we
don't see ourselves the way the devil says we are but
the way God says we are. He doesn't see our failures
and sin; He sees the blood of Jesus.

When you look in the mirror of God's Word, see
yourself the way your heavenly Father sees you. He
sees you healed, without sickness. He sees you free,
without bondage. He sees you full of joy, not sorrow.
He sees you a winner, not a loser.

The Lord asks us, "How do you plead?" We take a look at ourselves, forget what we saw in the mirror of God's Word, and say, "I plead guilty. I'm a drug addict, I'm an angry person, I'm depressed, and I'm no good." But the Lord whispers in our ear, "Don't plead guilty; plead the blood." When the Son sets us free, we are free indeed! We can tell every drug addict, every alcoholic, and every person with any problem that God has redeemed us and bought back our willpower.

The government has spent millions of dollars trying to help in the "Just Say No" program. Drug addicts, alcoholics, and people with depression and anger say "no" a hundred times a week, to no avail. Most people can't "just say no" in their own strength and willpower because they go back and do it again and again. They might not have any willpower in themselves, but in Jesus Christ their willpower has been ransomed and redeemed by the blood of the Lamb.

We recently received this testimony from a man who had given his life to the Lord but was still bound by uncontrollable habits until he claimed the blood of Jesus for his life.

> *Hello Pastor Huch,*
>
> *I want to write to you about the miracles and freedom that have taken place in my life after listening to your tape series "Breaking Family Curses." I have recently come to know Jesus Christ as my Savior and Redeemer. When the Holy Spirit came upon me, I saw my sins and the shame of what I had done. I was so ashamed that I wept. Until I found Jesus, I was truly on my way to hell.*

My father was a preacher who left his calling to become a hair stylist. He was drunk and on drugs all of the time and had many sexual relationships with both men and women. He would move out of the house for several months and then want to come back home. As a child I said, "I will never be like my father. I will never drink, never cheat on my wife, and never abandon my wife or child. I will never hit anyone, and I will never lie." My father was indeed a sinner, and the bondage he lived in was passed on to his five children.

I married the love of my heart, we had a child, and I became a deputy sheriff. I had fulfilled my childhood dream of becoming a law officer. I promised myself that I would be different from my father.

When I completed my year of job probation, my friends took me out to a bar for a celebration party. As soon as I took my first drink, something happened—the drink took me! I began to drink with the guys every day after my shift. I stayed away from home and began to have affairs with other women. I had become my father.

My wife, Julie, was diagnosed with breast cancer. She went through surgery, radiation, and chemotherapy to try to slow down the spread of this disease. Julie was an angel and loved God. In spite of her horrible cancer, she never complained or turned away from God. The day before she died, we sat together in the living room. She could not lift her head but kept looking up in the corners of the room. I asked her what she was looking at, and she said, "These angels are taking me to Jesus tonight." When she died later that night, I was out with another woman.

My life continued this horrible decline. All that my father was, I was, but worse. In 1998 the Holy Spirit of God knocked on the door of my soul and Jesus made Himself real to me. I was baptized in water, paid my tithes without failure, and read the Word of God. However, I was still in bondage.

Some friends told me they wanted me to hear your sermon on breaking family curses. The Holy Spirit of God came upon me as I listened, and I began to understand the blood of Jesus breaking the yokes of bondage of my father's sins and my sins. I had been redeemed, but I was not free. I claimed the blood of Jesus for my freedom just as God revealed to you. God broke the generational curse that had controlled my life!

I am free indeed. My child is free. The Holy Spirit of God is moving through my sister, and my brothers are calling to Jesus and asking to be free. My father is looking to God, and we are fighting in prayer for him daily.

All that I was is dead; all that I did is dead. I am no longer just living, but I am living for God. Jesus is my King. The Holy Spirit is my Comforter and my Driver. Your message revealed the true Word of God. I took back my freedom by the blood of Jesus, who paid the price and set me free on Calvary.

Pastor, thank you for teaching the Word of God and obeying God our Father.

Respectfully, your brother in Christ,
John

If you want to quit alcohol, drugs, or your violent anger and haven't been able to in the past, know that you can now. The blood of Jesus has bought back your willpower, and that curse on you is broken in the name of Jesus. You can quit drinking. You can quit smoking. You can quit doing those things you know God does not want you to do. Jesus has broken the curse of the past that keeps you from being free.

When you *choose* to break the curses on your life, the power of the blood of Jesus will strengthen you, and you will no longer be bound. You will be set free to do God's good work.

> *And I heard a loud voice saying in heaven, Now is come salvation, and strength, and the kingdom of our God, and the power of his Christ: for the accuser of our brethren is cast down, which accused them before our God day and night. And they overcame him by the blood of the Lamb.*
> (Revelation 12:10–11 KJV)

DISCUSSION QUESTIONS

1. (a) Where was the first place Jesus shed His blood?
   Read Luke 22:44. *In the garden - mt of Olives*

   (b) This is no coincidence. What did God tell Adam
   and Eve in Genesis 3:17? *They were cursed for disobeying God.*

2. The willpower we lost in the Garden of Eden was
   won back in the Garden of Gethsemane when Jesus
   said, "*Not as I will but as you will*."
   See the last part of Matthew 26:39.

3. The Bible says that Jesus prayed the same pray-
   er three times in the Garden of Gethsemane.
   What was the struggle going on inside Jesus?
   See Luke 22:43–46. *His human fears and His desire to do God's will.*

4. In Exodus 3:11–15, Moses questioned God about
   being chosen as the man who would lead the Israelites out of their captivity in Egypt.
   (a) In verse 13, what did Moses ask God?

   Who am I that I should go the Pharaoh + bring the Israelites out of Egypt.

(b) In verse 14, what name does God call Himself?

I am who I am

(c) Why do you think God called Himself by this name?

5. Read John 18:4–8 (KJV) and fill in the blanks.

Jesus therefore, knowing all things that should come upon him, went forth, and said unto them, Whom seek ye? They answered him, Jesus of Nazareth. Jesus saith unto them, ___I___ ___am___ ___He___. And Judas also, which betrayed him, stood with them. As soon then as he had said unto them, ___I___ ___am___ ___He___, they went backward, and fell to the ground. Then asked he them again, Whom seek ye? And they said, Jesus of Nazareth. Jesus answered, I have told you that ___I___ ___am___ ___He___: if therefore ye seek me, let these go their way.

6. What does James 1:23–25 say we sometimes do after going to the mirror (the Word of God) and seeing who we are?

We go away + don't do as we should.

CHAPTER 3

THE STRIPES ON JESUS' BACK WON BACK OUR HEALTH

But He was wounded for our transgressions,
He was bruised for our iniquities; the
chastisement for our peace was upon Him,
and by His stripes we are healed.
—Isaiah 53:5

The second place Jesus shed His blood was at the whipping post. It is believed that Jesus was scourged, or flogged, thirty-nine times. (See Matthew 27:26.) Under Jewish punishment, prisoners could be given forty lashes; however, they usually only received thirty-nine, because forty were often fatal. (See Deuteronomy 25:3.)

I heard a missionary doctor preach that the thirty-nine lashes represent all the categories of diseases known to all mankind. We need to remember that this is God's plan of redemption. It's not an accident or a coincidence, but it's His divine plan. Every time they laid the whip on Jesus' back—splitting His skin and ripping His muscles and tissue—healing was provided for every disease. AIDS, cancer, diabetes, muscular dystrophy, and every disease on this earth has been defeated and conquered by the blood of Jesus Christ. This shows God's willingness to heal everyone.

Some people say, "God doesn't heal anymore." But the Bible tells us, *"Jesus Christ is the same yesterday, today, and forever"* (Hebrews 13:8). Because He made a blood covenant, He doesn't change, and the blood covenant includes healing. Salvation doesn't just mean to be *forgiven*; it also means to be *healed*. Salvation means to be made whole in every way.

Others say, "We know God can heal, but does God *desire* to heal?" Keep in mind that Jesus willingly surrendered Himself to the whip! And many asked Jesus the same question while He walked the earth:

> *A man with leprosy came to him and begged him on his knees, "If you are willing, you can make me clean." Filled with compassion, Jesus reached out his hand and touched the man. "I am willing," he said. "Be clean!"*
> (Mark 1:40–41 NIV)

This man knew Jesus could heal him, but he wondered if He would heal him. One of the worst prayers we can pray is, "If it be Thy will, please heal me." The Bible tells us what the will of God is! If Jesus suffered the whip for our healing, of course it is His will we be healed. When we pray, *"If* it be Thy will," we're saying that we're not sure it's the will of God for us to be healed. But the Bible tells us to ask in rock-solid faith:

> *Let him ask in faith, nothing wavering. For he that wavereth is like a wave of the sea*

*driven with the wind and tossed. For let not
that man think that he shall receive any
thing of the Lord.*   (James 1:6–7 KJV)

To come boldly and confidently to God for healing is the opposite of saying, "If it be Thy will." If we
question God's will for us when we ask Him for something, we are double-minded—not asking in faith—
and He cannot heal us. Therefore, we must settle the
question, "Can God heal?" Yes! Absolutely! Not only
can God do anything, but our healing is so impor-
tant to Him that He made a covenant with us in the
blood of His Son. The price for your healing was paid
over two thousand years ago. All you have to do is
reach out and touch Jesus and receive your miracle.

I've preached in the Philippines many times,
and word would get around when we arrived that
the men of God were in town. We would get up in
the morning, and the sick, the blind, and the lame
would already be lined up along the street. We are
just normal human beings. We don't have the power
to heal ourselves, but people would come because
they heard the Word of God and they believed when
they heard, *"By His stripes we are healed"* (Isaiah
53:5). We would walk along the long lines of sick
people, touch them, lay hands on them, and pray for
them in the name of Jesus and by the power of His
blood. Then we would watch them get up and walk.
God still heals, saves, and delivers. We overcome the
devil and his infirmities by the blood of Jesus.

I'm often asked, "Pastor, why do we see so many
more miracles overseas than we do in the United
States or Europe?" Someone once said it's because
they have greater needs. I tend to disagree. If someone

is blind or lame or diseased, it doesn't matter if we're in South Carolina or South Africa—we need a miracle. Jesus taught us to come to Him as little children in order to see the kingdom of God—not just after we die, but now. Remember, Jesus told us to pray that His kingdom would come and His will would be done on earth as it is in heaven.

The apostle Paul declared in Romans 14:17 that the kingdom of God is righteousness, peace, and joy in the Holy Spirit. The apostle John declared in 3 John 1:2 that he wished we would prosper and be in health above everything else. When we get to heaven, we won't need any miracles. We need them now! We must trust God and believe for our healing now, when we need it. Other people on earth may fail us, even leave us, but our heavenly Father never will. When I get on an airplane, I have to have faith and trust in the pilot, crew, and everyone else involved in that flight. How much more can we trust the One who created the sky, the earth, and the sea? We must not waver or be double-minded, but trust God at His Word like little children and believe in the power of the blood of Jesus.

We received this letter from a woman who is still alive because of the healing stripes of Jesus Christ. The doctors gave her no chance to live after she was diagnosed with a terminal illness. We prayed for deliverance from the curse of infirmity that has been in her family, and she was miraculously healed.

Pastor Larry and Tiz,
I went to the doctor on January 18, and he said I was dying of Lou Gehrig's disease. I wrote

you a letter to pray for me. I went back to the doctor on February 26, and he said the disease is gone. I am now healed!

God has done this great miracle for me. I thank Him and praise Him now, today, tomorrow, forever, until He comes. He is my Father. Thank You, Jesus!

God bless you,
Sarah

A SPIRIT OF INFIRMITY

Our salvation starts with the forgiveness of our sin, but it doesn't stop there. It goes on to healing, deliverance, and freedom.

Now He was teaching in one of the synagogues on the Sabbath. And behold, there was a woman who had a spirit of infirmity eighteen years, and was bent over and could in no way raise herself up. But when Jesus saw her, He called her to Him and said to her, "Woman, you are loosed from your infirmity."   (Luke 13:10–12)

Here's a woman who, for eighteen years, walked around all bent over with a crippling disease. Jesus looked at her and said, "This woman has a spirit of sickness on her."

All sickness, no matter where it comes from—birth, inheritance, injury—is from the devil. Some people have told me they believe God will give a person cancer to test his or her love for Him. What God are you talking about? That is not my God! God can certainly use the circumstances of your sickness to accomplish His purposes, but He does not make you sick.

We read in Luke 12:32 that Jesus said, *"It is your Father's good pleasure to give you the kingdom."* It is the devil who steals, kills, and destroys. God gets pleasure by blessing those who believe in Him, not by sending sickness into their lives. There wasn't sickness or injury in the Garden of Eden. When Adam sinned, Satan entered the Garden, the curse came in, and that curse is an evil spirit.

Infirmity is a spirit that is a result of the curse, but everyone who is born again is redeemed from the curse. The price for your healing has been paid. If you are sick, injured, or diseased, Satan is trespassing on paid-for property. We don't need to say, "I need more faith to get my miracle." Instead, we can say, "By the blood of Jesus Christ, I have already received my miracle. Satan, I bind you from my life. Get out of my life! Leave me in the name of Jesus."

I was at a Bible conference some years ago, and people who wanted to be prayed for were standing in a line. We prayed for each person in the line, "In the name of Jesus, be healed." When I finished praying, I went back to a man I had already prayed for and asked him, "What's wrong with you?" He said that his hip socket was dissolving. He had been to the doctor earlier that day to have his hip X-rayed and tests done. Without thinking or even fully understanding what I was saying, I said, "That's a spirit of cancer. That's a demon of cancer." And we prayed for his deliverance.

A couple of weeks later, I was in Mexico with this man's pastor doing a miracle crusade. The pastor told me that after we had prayed for the man, he went back to get the results of his tests. The pastor then showed me a copy of the X-ray they took of this man's hip. As plain and as clear as a photo, we saw a complete face of a demonic-looking creature where the man's hipbone was supposed to be. Obviously startled by this, the man had asked the doctors about it. They told him that it was not totally uncommon to see something like this! In the end, however, the devil lost. The man was completely healed, and his hip was restored, praise God!

⌣ When we were in Australia, there was a Samoan woman in our church in Melbourne who had a tumor on her head the size of two golf balls. The doctors brought me into their office to talk to me because I was her pastor. Then I was to go and talk with her. I asked her doctor, "Where does cancer come from?"

He said, "Well, some will say one thing and some another. Some say it has to do with the red blood cells, and others will say it has to do with the white blood cells. To be honest with you, if we knew, we could fix it."

I told him, "Doctor, do you know what I think? I think it is a demonic spirit."

They looked at each other, and her doctor looked at me and said, "I wouldn't doubt it." That cancer was not just a sickness; it was alive.

One of the greatest miracles we've ever seen was when we prayed for this woman and God completely healed her. The tumors disappeared, the symptoms disappeared, and the doctors and nurses were astounded. Instead of sending her home to die, they sent her home to live!

When Jesus saw the woman who was bent over, He said, "You spirit...." Jesus spoke directly to the spirit. When I pray for healing from cancer, I don't say, "You sickness, be healed." I speak directly to the demon and say, "You come out of him right now in the name of Jesus." We see people healed of cancer all the time.

> *Then one of the crowd answered and said, "Teacher, I brought You my son, who has a mute spirit. And wherever it seizes him, it throws him down; he foams at the mouth, gnashes his teeth, and becomes rigid. So I spoke to Your disciples, that they should cast it out, but they could not." He answered him and said, "O faithless generation, how long shall I be with you? How long shall I bear with you? Bring him to Me." Then they brought him to Him. And when he saw Him, immediately the spirit convulsed him, and he fell on the ground and wallowed, foaming at the mouth. So He asked his father, "How long has this been happening to him?" And he said, "From childhood. And often he has thrown him both into the fire and into the water to destroy him. But if You can do anything, have compassion on us and help us." Jesus said to him, "If you can believe, all things are possible to him who believes." Immediately the father of the child cried out and said with tears, "Lord, I believe; help my unbelief!" When Jesus saw that the people came running together, He rebuked the unclean spirit, saying to it, "Deaf and dumb*

spirit, I command you, come out of him and enter him no more!" Then the spirit cried out, convulsed him greatly, and came out of him. And he became as one dead, so that many said, "He is dead." But Jesus took him by the hand and lifted him up, and he arose. (Mark 9:17–27)

Jesus didn't offer up some eloquent prayer for the child. He spoke directly to the demon. Jesus called that spirit by name and commanded it to leave that boy.

In Mark 5:25–34, we find the story about a certain woman who had an issue of blood for twelve years. *"She had suffered a great deal under the care of many doctors and had spent all she had, yet instead of getting better she grew worse"* (Mark 5:26 NIV). This woman had seen every doctor available and had spent all her money on medical care, yet she was worse than when this infirmity began. When she heard about Jesus coming to town, *"she thought, 'If I just touch his clothes, I will be healed'"* (Mark 5:28 NIV). And when she touched the hem of His garment, immediately the bleeding stopped, and she was healed.

Jesus knew right away that power had gone out of Him. He looked around Him and asked His disciples, *"Who touched me?"* (Mark 5:31 NIV). Now, there was a large crowd that had gathered around, and people all around Him were touching Him. But Jesus knew that one particular person had touched Him in faith, causing power and anointing to be released. Fearfully, the woman fell at Jesus' feet and admitted that it was she who had touched His cloak.

He said to her, "Daughter, your faith has healed you. Go in peace and be freed from your suffering." (Mark 5:34 NIV)

Remember that this illness had stolen her health and all of her living. When she touched Jesus and was made whole, I believe that not only was she healed physically, but that, through her faith, God restored everything financially that the disease had taken from her. Is it the will of God for you to be healed? Yes, because by His stripes we are healed. (See Isaiah 53:5.) The word *stripe* means "the blow that cuts."[5] The suffering for sickness and disease has already been paid by the shed blood of Jesus Christ.

GOD STILL HEALS TODAY

Don't be discouraged if someone you know isn't healed yet. Be motivated. There are people in my family who need to be saved. I'm not condemned or discouraged by that; I am motivated because I know God is still working. He is not finished.

Not too long ago in the first service at our church, the presence of God was absolutely marvelous. As we were worshipping the Lord, I began to weep from the presence of God. I knew God was doing something very, very special. In our second service, I never even got to preach. Instead, I began to call people through the word of wisdom and the word of knowledge. In one case, the Lord showed me there was a woman who had a lump on her breast, and that she was not to worry, because He had just healed her.

We received a phone call a couple of days later from a woman who lived in California. As she was watching our television program, God said to her to come to our church that Sunday and she would get the miracle that she'd been seeking. On Monday, she was to have her breast operated on because of cancer. She told us that before they operated, they needed to take one more X-ray. When they did, they found nothing! They X-rayed her two more times and said, "Get up and get dressed. There is no reason to operate." Glory to God, the Great Physician worked again!

A couple of days after that, a lady in our church who also had a lump in her breast told us that when I said God was healing that problem, the lump in her breast completely dissolved. God is still a miracle-working God!

After Jesus shed His blood in the Garden of Gethsemane, He went to the whipping post. When they tied Jesus to the whipping post, they whipped Him thirty-nine times with a whip consisting of several leather thongs, each loaded with jagged pieces of metal or bone and weighted at the end with lead. With each strike of the whip, flesh was torn and blood came out of the back of our Savior. Every single time the devil put the whip to Jesus' back, blood was shed, and we overcame one disease, two diseases, three diseases, until the point that every sickness brought on mankind was conquered by the blood of Jesus. No longer do you have to live under the curse of sickness and disease. You have been set free by the precious blood of Jesus!

DISCUSSION QUESTIONS

1. Some people say God doesn't heal anymore and that He healed people only during biblical times. But what does the Bible say about Jesus Christ in Hebrews 13:8? *He is the same yesterday today + forever*

2. Others believe God can heal but question His desire to do so. Many people asked Jesus about His willingness to heal. What did He answer the man with leprosy in Mark 1:40–41 (NIV)? *moved with pity. He said. "I will."*

3. How does the Bible say we should ask in James 1:6–7 (KJV)? *In faith - not doubting.*

4. (a) What does Isaiah 53:5 say about our healing? *by His wounds we are healed*

   (b) What does the apostle John declare in 3 John 1:2 about healing? *prayed for good health*

5. Read Luke 13:10–12 and answer the following questions:
   (a) What kind of spirit did the woman have on her? *disabling*

(b) What did Jesus say to the woman?

You are freed from your disability

6. Another dramatic healing took place in Mark 9:17–27.
   (a) What kind of spirit was on the boy?

   Made him mute, + caused seizures

   (b) Could Jesus' disciples cast the spirit out of the boy? *No*

   (c) What did Jesus say about the importance of belief in verse 23? *All things are possible if you believe*

7. Read Mark 5:25–34.
   (a) What do verses 27–28 say the woman with the issue of blood did when Jesus came to town? *Got close to Him + touched Him.*

   (b) What happened to her? *She was healed of her disease.*

Jesus' Crown of Thorns Won Back Our Prosperity

We are redeemed by the precious blood of Jesus. Through His blood, we have been brought back to the state Adam and Eve enjoyed in the Garden of Eden. They lived in the blessing and the presence of God. There was no sickness or poverty. When Adam was obeying God, he had everything he needed. Adam and Eve literally lived in the land that flowed with milk and honey. But when Adam disobeyed God, God declared the curse that came upon the land through Adam's sin.

> *Because you have heeded the voice of your wife, and have eaten from the tree of which I commanded you, saying, "You shall not eat of it": Cursed is the ground for your sake; in toil you shall eat of it all the days of your life. Both thorns and thistles it shall bring forth for you, and you shall eat the herb of the field. In the sweat of your face you shall eat bread till you return to the ground.*
>
> (Genesis 3:17–19)

God cursed the ground with thorns and thistles. If we don't understand that we've been redeemed
from the curse by the blood of Jesus, then the land
we go to work in, the land we build our businesses
in, and the land we live in is still under a curse.
When Adam sinned, no longer could he live in God's
abundance and splendor. The land was cursed, and
by the sweat of his brow, man would eke out an existence. Since that day, mankind has sweated for
everything it has gotten. But the third place Jesus
shed His blood broke the curse of poverty.

Thousands of years after Adam sinned, Jesus
Christ, the second Adam, was taken before the religious and political authorities to stand trial as a
fraud and a heretic. On the way to Pilate, as they
were mocking Jesus, "All hail, King of the Jews,"
they saw a thorn bush—the symbol of the curse of
poverty on the land. They took some of the thorn
branches, wove them into a crown, and placed them
on the brow of Jesus until the blood flowed from His
head. (See Matthew 27:29.)

The symbol of poverty was placed on the brow of
Jesus, the second Adam. When those thorns pierced
His brow, He shed His blood for our redemption from
poverty. We were cursed with poverty by the sweat of
Adam's brow, but we were redeemed from the curse
of poverty by the blood on Jesus' brow.

What Satan means for evil, God will use for
good. (See Genesis 50:20.) The soldiers took that
crown of thorns and placed it on Jesus' head. Instead
of sweat, out poured the blood of Jesus. Now, by the
power of the blood of Jesus, not only is the curse of

poverty broken, but those who take the name of Jesus and claim His blood are anointed to prosper.

For you know the grace of our Lord Jesus Christ, that though He was rich, yet for your sakes He became poor, that you through His poverty might become rich.

(2 Corinthians 8:9)

Jesus was never poor. When the Bible says Jesus became poor, it means He was poor in comparison to what He had in His heavenly home. In heaven the streets are made of pure gold, walls and gates are made of precious gems, and there's not one poverty bone in all of God's body. When someone reads that Jesus became poor, He was poor in relationship to how He lived in heaven. If you were to take all the money in the world and give it to one man, that one man would be a poor man in comparison to what Jesus had in heaven before He became a human being on earth. Even on earth, Jesus may have refused material goods while He was preaching, but He could have called down the angels at any time to provide for His needs.

A man said to me one time, "Jesus was poor, and I want to be just like Jesus." I asked him why he thought Jesus was poor. He said Jesus was poor because He was born in a manger, and this was to show us that we don't need worldly riches. Yes, Jesus was born in a manger, but not to teach us poverty. He was showing us that we were not making room for the Savior to be born in our lives.

Before Mary and Joseph went to the barn, they first went to the inn to get a room. I doubt if Mary was going to put the charge on one of her credit cards or that she intended to sneak out of the window in the morning without paying the bill. Mary and Joseph had plenty of money to get a room at the inn. The problem was that the inn had no room for the Savior.

Nevertheless, we have religiously and traditionally taught that Jesus was poor, so Christians should be poor. Christmas programs usually show three wise men around the manger with their little gifts: small boxes of gold, frankincense, and myrrh. A friend of mine researched the three wise men and their gifts. He discovered that gold was not the only priceless gift they offered Christ. Frankincense and myrrh are also precious substances. Furthermore, according to Matthew 2:1, there could have been many wise men. These gifts could have ensured that Jesus and His family lived in comfort.

When I teach this, I always ask people, "How many know that the Word of God is the most powerful thing on earth?" Everybody always shouts, "Amen!" Then I shock them by saying, "But it's not. The Bible says that man's religious traditions make the Word of God of no effect." (See Mark 7:13.) So, in order to avoid making the Word of God powerless and impotent in our lives, we must beware not to fall into lifeless, religious thinking and traditions— which is one of the wiles of the devil.

Paul taught us to beware of the wiles of the devil, which means we must understand his strategies, the ways he will attempt to ambush us. One of his greatest wiles is used to keep us poor. If he can get us to believe that Jesus lived in poverty and that to be like Jesus we must live in poverty, then he has trapped us and the Word of God—*"I have come that they may have life, and that they may have it more abundantly"*

(John 10:10)—becomes ineffective in our lives. The devil's strategy is to make us speak the tradition of men so that we should be poor and shut our mouths to the Word of God that in Christ Jesus we are rich.

There are a couple of times in the Bible when Jesus would touch someone and say, "Now, don't tell anybody." And what would that person do? Immediately, he would run off and tell everybody. I have to believe that Jesus would just laugh to Himself. He knew no one could keep his mouth shut. They are like my brother Norm when he got saved—I mean really saved—a couple of months ago. Now, all he wants to talk about is Jesus. He tells everybody what Jesus did for him and has already started a Bible study in his home. Norm didn't get a religion; he got a relationship with the Son of God. Norm is just like these people in the Bible. When Jesus touched them, they couldn't stop talking about Him. The devil knows this, too! He knows we're going to tell as many people as we can that no matter what we're going through, no matter what we need, Jesus will meet that need. The devil's strategy is to get us to believe the lie that we're supposed to be poor so we won't be able to afford to get the good news out.

I used to believe in the poverty doctrine. I believed it, I preached it, and, believe me, it worked! Then, one day Tiz and I met John Avanzini, a man of God who changed our lives. God was stirring us about prosperity, but our traditions were battling with the Word of God. Finally I said to John, "I really want to know the truth. So if I say anything that's wrong, just tell me and show it to me in the Word." I then began to tell him why I thought it was wrong for us to prosper and have nice things. Immediately, John said, "Larry, you're wrong."

"Why?" I asked.

"You think that, instead of Christians having a nice home or a nice car or a nice church, this money ought to be used to win the world to Jesus."

"Yes," I said, "exactly."

What John told me next has changed my life, my ministry, and my family forever. He said, "Larry, God's not on a budget; He owns it all. He has enough money to win the world a thousand times over and still see all of His children blessed above anything they could ask or think."

Proverbs 13:22 says, *"A good man leaves an inheritance to his children's children, but the wealth of the sinner is stored up for the righteous."* Do you know what that verse means? Not only are we supposed to be so wealthy that we leave an inheritance to our grandchildren, but God is trying to get the wealth of the world into the hands of the church. Every good thing comes from our Father above, including the wisdom and provision for houses, cars, clothing— and for preaching the Gospel to every creature on the earth. The wealth of this earth is for God's children.

We have a blood covenant with Jesus to move us from poverty into prosperity, but look at the abundance that is out in the world. Unbelievers have got our stuff! God knows we have need of all these things. So, we must rise up and tell our Father, "We're ready for our stuff now!"

We must realize that acquiring goods is not the goal. True riches are not material. However, if we ask

God to provide salvation, healing, or help in times of trouble, can we not rely on Him to provide us with the means to pay our bills? Then we can take good care of our families and bless the world with the Gospel of Jesus Christ.

⌒ IS POVERTY OF GOD OR OF THE DEVIL?

Some people believe that wealth is of the devil and that God wants Christians to be poor, but James 1:13 tells us that God can tempt no man with evil. If money and prosperity were evil, then God never would have given us promises of blessings in return for our tithes.

> *"Bring all the tithes into the storehouse, that there may be food in My house, and try Me now in this," says the LORD of hosts, "if I will not open for you the windows of heaven and pour out for you such blessing that there will not be room enough to receive it. And I will rebuke the devourer for your sakes, so that he will not destroy the fruit of your ground, nor shall the vine fail to bear fruit for you in the field," says the LORD of hosts; "and all nations will call you blessed, for you will be a delightful land," says the LORD of hosts.* (Malachi 3:10–12)

The *New International Version* translates "*windows*" as "*floodgates.*" The floodgates hold back the flood. If we believe that prosperity is not of God and rob Him of our tithes and offerings, the floodgates remain closed, and we are unable to experience the blessings He has for us. I don't know about you, but I like the idea of God pouring out so much blessing on me that I don't have enough room to contain it!

The word "*windows*" also is derived from the word *ambush*.[6] God wants to ambush us with prosperity! I believe He has to ambush us, or sneak up on us, because we have been taught that poverty and Christianity are synonymous.

Tiz and I have never missed giving of our tithes in all the years we've been saved. We have never made a pledge and not paid it. But we never saw the financial blessing and prosperity of God until we realized that poverty is part of a curse from which we've been redeemed. Poverty is not God's will; prosperity is God's will.

> *Give, and it will be given to you: good measure, pressed down, shaken together, and running over will be put into your bosom. For with the same measure that you use, it will be measured back to you.* (Luke 6:38)

God doesn't want us to live out of the bottom of the barrel. He wants our houses paid for, our cars paid for, our churches paid for, and enough money to evangelize the world. God is not broke. He owns the cattle on a thousand hills. (See Psalm 50:10.) The earth is the Lord's and the fullness thereof, and we are heirs to that covenant promise. (See Psalm 50:12.)

Let's see what else the Word of God has to say about prosperity.

> *The wealth of the sinner is stored up for the righteous.* (Proverbs 13:22)

> *You shall remember the* LORD *your God, for
> it is He who gives you power to get wealth,
> that He may establish His covenant.*
> (Deuteronomy 8:18)

> *And God is able to make all grace abound
> toward you, that you, always having all
> sufficiency in all things, may have an abun-
> dance for every good work.*
> (2 Corinthians 9:8)

Poverty is not part of Christianity. *Prosperity* is part of Christianity. Prosperity is part of God's redemption plan for His people. We need to remember that we are spirits who live in bodies, and we function through our souls—our emotions and intellect. As a man *"thinks in his heart, so is he"* (Proverbs 23:7). So if we think poverty is part of Christianity, then poverty stays with us. But when we understand that we are redeemed from poverty by the blood of Jesus, we can be set free and receive the prosperity God has for us.

There are teachings in pulpits across the nation that prosperity is not of God, but don't forget that money turns on the lights! Money feeds kids in Cambodia. Money supports our foreign missionaries as they present the Gospel to the lost. Money supports the orphanages. Money means we can reach the kids on the streets.

Don't listen to anyone who teaches that God wants you to be poor and needy. If you listen to it, you're going to absorb it, and it is scripturally wrong. God has reversed the curse.

> *Blessed is the man who walks not in the
> counsel of the ungodly.*   (Psalm 1:1)

Be careful who you listen to. The blood that Jesus shed when they pressed the crown of thorns on His head has reversed the curse of poverty. All you have to do to move out of poverty and into prosperity is believe that the blood of Jesus has reversed the curse, accept His promise of prosperity for your life, and obey God in giving.

I was teaching this in the Philippines and a pastor said to me, "Well, that's okay for you guys, but we're not in America." The Bible is not a book written solely for Americans. The Word of God is not exclusive to a certain race or a certain nation. The Bible was written for *all* people. So I said to this pastor, "How can you say prosperity is not for you? You can see prosperity at work when your cows have two calves instead of one. You see your fishermen bring in an abundance like Peter did when he fished and the nets were full and the fish were large yet the nets didn't break. And you've seen your rice crops yield double the amount of what was expected."

Our idea of prosperity can be so limited. Don't limit God! Recognize the prosperity of God in your life and be thankful.

WORK IS NOT A CURSE

Do we have to work? Yes, we have to work. In this world, it is a day's work for a day's wage. However, God multiplies our work. The work it takes the world to bring in a year of harvest, God can bring to His children in a month. What takes the world ten years to earn, God can bring to us in six months. The world functions by the law of poverty, by the sweat of their brow, but you and I function by the law of redemption, by the blood of His brow, and that curse of poverty has been broken.

Work itself is not the curse because Adam worked before the curse. The Bible says that if you don't work, you don't eat. (See 2 Thessalonians 3:10.) You can't be saying, "Oh, God, meet my need," and your relatives and friends are asking, "Why aren't you working?"

"Well, I'm living by faith," you answer.

No, if you are able to work and are not working, you are living by mooch, not by faith! Living by faith does not mean you don't have to work. *Living by faith is working and believing God will bless your labor.* Don't tell people, "Well, I don't work because I live by faith and I know God will provide." That is *not* God's faith. Welfare may provide, but welfare is for people who *can't* work, not for people who *won't* work. Seek God's wisdom, delight yourself in the Lord, meditate in His Word day and night, work diligently in everything, and whatever you do God will prosper. (See Psalm 1:1–3; Proverbs 10:3–4.)

FRUITLESS LABOR

Adam was living in abundance when he was tending the Garden, and God multiplied Adam's abundance through his labor. Things were growing and flourishing. But when Adam disobeyed God, the ground was cursed, and instead of bubbling with provision, Adam had to work to pry out that provision. Instead of automatically yielding fruit, herbs, and trees, the ground yielded thorns and thistles. Hard work, labor, and sweat became a way of life just to survive.

Before the curse, Adam was blessed as he toiled. God blessed his work, and it yielded great abundance. However, when the curse came, the ground that once yielded abundance was cursed and Adam had to work hard in order to barely get by.

This is where most of us live. We have to pry out an existence because the earth we live on is cursed. *But we have been redeemed from that curse by the blood of the Lamb.* God has provided a way for us to break the curse of poverty.

A woman wrote to us after watching our television program and hearing that curses are broken by the blood of Jesus Christ. She found hope for her family who had been afflicted by poverty for five generations.

> *Dear Pastor Huch,*
>
> *We are a hardworking people, but we can never get any further than working hard. No matter how many jobs I have at one time, I cannot seem to save that "nest egg." Something always seems to come up, whereby I have to use that little money saved to pay for something else. I would like to see my entire family with property of their own and money for retirement years, instead of working until the body grows old and becomes ready for the grave.*
>
> *To my knowledge, there have been five generations of terrible marriages, divorce, and lack. I hate the poverty in my life, in my family's life, and in this city. When I heard your message on TBN, I was thrilled. Although I did not have a label for the problems, I have always known there must be*

something terribly wrong because of the poverty, divorces, and single parents in our family.

Pastor Huch, I grieve for my family, for myself, and for the city in which I live. It doesn't have to continue this way, and I rejoice in the knowledge that it can and will change.

I was watching your program one Sunday afternoon on TBN. The Lord gave me that moment to view your program, so I know He wanted me to seek your ministry. Please pray for me and all that I have shared with you.

Sincerely yours,
Sonja

I've heard a lot of people say, "I believe God will bless us in the sweet by-and-by and give us the pie-in-the-sky-when-we-die." But God also wants us to have it here on the ground while we're still around! You can't bless the world if your prosperity is in the sky. Prosperity means that as you're doing your work, as you're doing your job, as you're running your business or building your church, you are doing it all for God. God said, "I get involved, and I don't move by the world's ways; I move by supernatural ways, and I prosper you in the journey."

We sometimes limit God because our idea of prosperity conforms to the world's idea of prosperity. A person may give up everything to become a missionary in a third-world country yet still be prosperous. How is this possible? Because God will provide the plane ticket to get there, will supply Bibles and medical supplies for the people, and will multiply your work so that a whole village can be saved. God may not give you a Rolls-Royce, but He will make sure your clothes don't wear out, as He did for the Israelites as they wandered in the desert, until you get that raise you've been asking for. Prosperity is manna in the desert because a priceless ruby isn't going to feed your empty belly. God knows what you need.

A lady in our church ran up to me the other day and said, "Pastor, thank you for teaching on breaking the curse of poverty and living in prosperity! I want you to know I'm the first person in the history of our family to purchase a house. The spirit of poverty is broken off my life and my children's lives, and I am a proud homeowner. Praise be to God!"

A couple came and told me they had been $14,000 in debt with a hospital bill from an unexpected illness and that they were close to losing their home. Their mother heard the message of God's supernatural debt cancellation and said to God, "You mean You can get my kids out of debt?" So she began to pray. Shortly afterward, the hospital called this couple and said, "We're going to cancel your debt. It's paid in full." They are blessed, and the kingdom of God is blessed through them because they obeyed God and gave their tithes and offerings out of the money that was restored to them.

DON'T LOSE WHAT YOU ALREADY HAVE

The blessing from God is not just what is out in front of you, but also what is not overtaking you from behind. Part of the curse of poverty is that the devourer tries to overtake you from behind. Being devoured means you start to get ahead and your car breaks down; you start to get ahead and your kids get sick and you have a hospital bill; you start to get ahead and some other bill comes along and drains your reserve.

If you are paying your tithes and giving offerings, God *"will rebuke the devourer for your sakes"* (Malachi 3:11). There are times when the devil is going to try to cause your car to break down and your engine to blow up. Then God intervenes and says, "No, don't touch that, because he's paid his tithe and the curse of poverty is reversed."

God said, "All the world will see you and say, 'They are blessed of the Lord.'" (See Malachi 3:12.) When you have a nice home and car, and your wife and children are dressed nicely, the world says, "They are blessed." Your life reflects the nature of God. You represent His goodness and blessing.

For fifteen years, Tiz and I witnessed to our family about the Lord, but they wouldn't listen to a word we said. We had sold out for God, were buying our clothes at thrift stores, driving pieces of junk, and just barely able to make ends meet. They would ask us, "If you're working for God so much, why doesn't He take care of you?" That made sense! We were preaching the Gospel while living in poverty and bragging about it! "C'mon, join us, lose everything. C'mon. Where is everyone? C'mon. What's wrong with you? Don't you want to be in constant need like us?" Then we learned that God wants to bless His children.

> *Let them shout for joy and be glad, who favor my righteous cause; and let them say continually, "Let the Lord be magnified,*

*who has pleasure in the prosperity of His
servant."*   (Psalm 35:27)

My giving has quadrupled because God prospers everything I put my hands to. If you are already
tithing, all you have to do is accept what the blood
has done and say, "I apply the blood of the Lamb to
my job, my finances, and my family."

There is a lot of controversy over the prosperity message. I agree that there has been misuse and
abuse by some, but that doesn't change the Word
of God. I know some people say, "Well, we've seen
people backslide once they gained money and material things." So have I. But I've seen a lot more backslide because they were sick and tired of "paying the
price," and "suffering for Jesus," and working year
after year with nothing to show for it.

Poverty is part of the curse. God never intended for His children to live in poverty. God never intended for His children to be the "scourge of society."
From the beginning, God's intention for His beloved
children has been blessing and prosperity. In Deuteronomy 28:1–14, God tells His people the results
of serving Him wholeheartedly—blessing, blessing,
blessing!

Probably the greatest lie that Satan has ever
pulled off was that poverty is an indicator of godli-
ness. If Christians are bound financially, they have
very little to give to their church. If the churches are
bound financially, they have very little to do their
work. Consequently, the work of God is slowed down
or stopped completely. Missionaries can't be sent out.
Bibles can't be printed. People say the Gospel is free.

Yes, the message is free, but it takes lots of money to accomplish God's vision. The good news is that He is our Source and our Provider.

I taught this message in a foreign church that had been supported by American mission money for fifty-three years. They accepted the fact that Jesus shed His blood for our prosperity and the curse of poverty on them was broken. Not only did they not need missionary money any longer, but within a year they launched three of their own churches.

There is an end-time harvest of souls that is beginning to take place. God is bringing an end-time transfer of wealth to His people so we can fulfill His plans. We need to get positioned to move from poverty to prosperity. We've got to get positioned in our minds, in our spirits, and in our actions to receive what God wants to do in our lives.

God is not against us having money. He is against money having us. If we keep God and His work first priority in our lives, there's no end to the prosperity He'll pour to us and through us. God is not asking us to take a *vow of poverty*, but He is asking us to take a *vow of priorities*. As we are faithful in our finances in the natural realm, God will multiply and pour out finances in the supernatural realm.

Read this testimony from Suzanne, one of our members at New Beginnings Christian Center, who broke the curse of poverty in her life and is living in God's prosperity.

Pastor Huch and Tiz,
The teaching I have received in the last six years of attending New Beginnings has had a large part in the person I am today.

When I arrived in Portland six years ago,
I was homeless. Six years of a very physically and
emotionally abusive marriage left me fearful and
with little self-esteem. I lived in shelters for battered
women and started attending New Beginnings.

I was put in "the system" on welfare and low-
income housing. I got off welfare, and my children
and I lived on child support of $423 a month. I had
no job skills, had never finished high school, and
had not worked in six years. I had my talent as an
artist, and I tithed, even when I lived in poverty.

In November 1996, I asked God to be my
business partner. I said my life was His—I would
do whatever He asked. All of this time I have been
reading His Word, listening to tapes, and growing.
In 1996, my gross income from my art was under
$8,000. In 1997, I started praying "specifically,"
just as you taught us to do. In January, I prayed
I would make $6,000, and it happened! Then I
prayed that I could double it. In March, I grossed
$12,000.

I lived in low-income housing and wanted
to move, so I prayed God would give me enough
money to buy a house. In September, I grossed over
$20,000 in a thirty-five-day period and bought a
home on a contract.

Then I said, "God, I need a new van. This
one is no longer safe." A week later, I had a new
van. I now have a successful business where I can
gross $10,000-plus a month. I now make $500-
plus a day—more than I used to live on in a
month. I believe this year my tithe will be more
than I used to live on in a year.

My mind-set has been changed through the
messages I have received in church and through

tapes and books. Everything you are teaching works, if people would just do it. I'm working very hard, but I'm also faithful to attend and stay involved in church. I know I have to stay connected to my source.

"He raiseth up the poor out of the dust, and lifteth the needy out of the dunghill; that he may set him with princes, even with the princes of his people" *(Psalm 113:7–8 KJV). My clients are some of the wealthiest, most powerful people in the state, and they are willing to wait in line for me to work for them. I just turned thirty years old the other day, and my life has only just begun. Thank you.*

God bless,
Suzanne

Our God is the Lord of the harvest! What He has done for Suzanne, He can and wants to do for you! Poverty no longer has a place in your life because that curse has been broken. It was broken when the crown of thorns pierced Jesus' sinless head and His sinless blood poured down His body. If you need a job, seek the Lord. I believe you will receive a job that you will not only love, but that will also pay you above and beyond what you need. And as you receive God's blessings, you can turn around and be a blessing to others. You cannot out-give God!

DISCUSSION QUESTIONS

1. In Genesis 3:17–19, what did God tell Adam would happen because of his disobedience?

   He would have to work for His provision

2. On the way to Pilate, as the soldiers were mocking Jesus, what did they place on His head? See Matthew 27:29. *Crown of thorns*

3. What does Genesis 50:20 say about Satan's plans?

   Satan planned evil but God planned for good

4. In 2 Corinthians 8:9, what does it say you become as a result of Christ taking your poverty on Himself? *rich*

5. What does Mark 7:13 say about religious traditions?

6. When it comes to the devil, Paul taught us to be aware of what? See Ephesians 6:11.

   The schemes of the devil

7. Proverbs 13:22 says, *"A good man leaves an inheritance to his children's children, but the wealth*

of a sinner is stored up for the righteous." What do you think this verse means?

8. Some people believe that wealth is of the devil and that God wants Christians to be poor. What does James 1:13 tell us? God doesn't tempt us with evil

9. Read Malachi 3:10–12 and fill in the blanks below:

   "Bring all the ___tithe___ *into the storehouse, that there may be food in My house, and try Me now in this," says the* LORD *of hosts, "if I will not open for you the* ___windows___ *of heaven and pour out for you such blessing that there will not be room enough to receive it. And I will rebuke the* ___devourer___ *for your sakes, so that he will not destroy the fruit of your ground, nor shall the vine fail to bear fruit for you in the field," says the* LORD *of hosts; "and all nations will call you* ___blessed___ *, for you will be a delightful land," says the* LORD *of hosts.*

10. What do the following Scriptures tell you about prosperity?
    (a) Luke 6:38 Give + it will be given to you. Running over

(b) Proverbs 13:22 *Sinner stores up for himself & recieves no inheritance*

(c) Deuteronomy 8:18 *The Lord gives power to have wealth*

(d) 2 Corinthians 9:8 *abundance for every good deed*

11. Have you ever wondered why we need to work and how work fits into the prosperity God has for His people? Do you believe that work itself is part of the curse Adam brought on the world?

12. What does God say in Deuteronomy 28:1–14 are the results of serving Him wholeheartedly?

    Obey the Lord - blessings abound

13. Turn again to Deuteronomy 28:1–14 and pray the verses out loud, inserting your own name every place it says, "*thee*," "*thou*," or "*thine*."

CHAPTER 5

JESUS' PIERCED HANDS WON BACK DOMINION OVER THE THINGS WE TOUCH

The fourth place Jesus' blood was shed was from His hands, where the soldiers pounded spikes to nail Him to the cross. I believe that through the blood shed from His nail-pierced hands, God says everything we put our hands to He will cause to prosper. (See Genesis 39:3.)

Before the fall of Adam, you and I were created by God to be in charge of and to have dominion over all the earth.

> Then God said, "Let Us make man in Our image, according to Our likeness; let them have dominion over the fish of the sea, over the birds of the air, and over the cattle, over all the earth and over every creeping thing that creeps on the earth." So God created man in His own image; in the image of God He created him; male and female He created them. Then God blessed them, and God said to them, "Be fruitful and multiply; fill the earth and subdue it; have dominion over

72

the fish of the sea, over the birds of the air, and over every living thing that moves on the earth." (Genesis 1:26–28)

God placed all authority in the hands of Adam and Eve, but when Adam disobeyed God, that authority was taken from us, and Satan became the god of this world. Satan began to take charge. I believe that, when Jesus was crucified, He shed His blood as they drove spikes into His hands so you and I would regain our dominion and become overcomers. Our authority has been redeemed through the shed blood of Jesus' hands.

Many Christians are running away from the devil or trying to hide from him. We think that if we run fast enough and speak in tongues enough, the devil won't get us too badly. Then there are other Christians who are holding ground and think the devil will ignore them if they just keep quiet and don't make too much noise.

As Christians, we are not to be timid, be on the defensive, or operate in neutral. We can overcome the devil. We can defeat the devil. We can have victory over the enemy of our lives who is out to destroy us. We can go after the attacks of Satan and defeat them. We can take the offensive to thwart the enemy's tactics against us.

Lay Hold of What Belongs to God

Even the world notices when the Lord causes His people to prosper. For example, Potiphar observed that although Joseph was a slave, he was successful and prosperous and *"the Lord made all he did to prosper in his hand"* (Genesis 39:3). That is why the devil doesn't want you to lay your hands on things and take authority over what belongs to God and His people.

Once when I was preaching in Michigan, we laid hands on and prayed for a woman who needed a double blessing. This is the testimony she later sent to us.

> *Dear Pastor Huch,*
>
> *I came to see you when you were in Detroit. What a wonderful and anointed message on breaking the curse of financial debt you preached. The Lord spoke to me, and it was confirmed that I would be doubly blessed. After you asked who would like to receive the laying on of hands for the release of the anointing, I ran forward with everyone else. You laid hands on me twice.*
>
> *Over a month later, I became pregnant, which I have been praying about for over three-and-a-half years. On the very same day I found out I was pregnant, my husband received a $50,000-a-year job. For the past two years, he had been unemployed. Through it all, the Lord has sustained us and met our every need.*
>
> *I will continue to believe that during this Jubilee year, the Lord will take care of all our financial debts we have acquired over these years of unemployment. Thanks to your teaching on breaking generational curses, I am able to receive God's promise for a pain-free delivery of this blessed and healthy baby I am carrying.*
>
> *God bless,*
> *Jamilla*

When Jesus bled from His hands, dominion was returned to God's children. That means that whatever evil we encounter, we have the authority in Jesus' name to render it harmless.

They will take up serpents; and if they drink anything deadly, it will by no means hurt them; they will lay hands on the sick, and they will recover.　　　　(Mark 16:18)

You need to lay hands on your children, cover them with the blood of Jesus, and say, "I break the iniquity off my kids. I break the iniquity off my family." You need to lay hands on your children's pillows and declare that they are going to serve God. You need to lay your hands on your children's school and cover it with the blood of Jesus. If you have an unsaved husband, lay your hands on your husband's pillow and release the anointing of the Spirit of God. Take authority over those demons of iniquity and, all of a sudden, Dad is going to start opening the Bible and reading it. He said he would never go to church, but now he's getting the whole family to go. Why? Because the iniquity is broken by the blood of Jesus the moment you take authority over the enemy and the Holy Spirit is loosed to bring God's promises to pass in your life.

Everything you put your hands to, God will cause to prosper. (See Genesis 39:3.) Why? Not because it's a ritual but because authority has been returned to our hands through the precious blood of Jesus.

When we were pastoring a church in Santa Fe, a large building was being renovated downtown for a homosexual and lesbian disco. We got our church members together, went down there, laid hands on the building, and said, "You foul spirit, we bind you, we take dominion over this place, and we declare that it will not open."

On the day of the grand opening, all the electricity blew up, so it had to be shut down. Repairs were made and another grand opening was scheduled. We went back to the building, laid hands on it, and said, "You foul spirit, in the name of Jesus, we take dominion over you. You are not going to rise up in this city for immoral purposes." They were set to open and something else blew up. This went on for a year-and-a-half while millions of dollars were spent and went down the drain. It never did open. Was this simply a coincidence? Absolutely not!

IT'S REAL!

We are to have authority. God gave us authority in the Garden of Eden, we lost it through Adam's sin, and Jesus redeemed it on the cross. Jesus laid His hands down. He didn't resist His opponents; He just laid His body down, and they drove those spikes into His hands. His blood was shed, and dominion came back into the hands of all who believe in Him.

The Word of God says we have been redeemed by the blood of Jesus. Our authority has been redeemed. Our dominion has been redeemed. We need to take our hands, lay them on everything, and claim the blessings of God with authority, by the blood and in the name of Jesus Christ!

DISCUSSION QUESTIONS

1. Read Genesis 1:26–28 and list all the things God gave man dominion over. *fish, birds, cattle every creeping thing*

2. In Genesis 39:3, what did Potiphar observe about the slave Joseph? *The Lord caused him to prosper*

3. According to Mark 16:17–18, what signs follow those who believe in Jesus' name? *Cast out demons, speak in tongues, pick up serpents, lay hands on the sick*

4. The Word of God says we have been redeemed by the blood of Jesus. Our authority has been redeemed. Our dominion has been redeemed. Take your hands right now, lay them on everything, and claim the blessings of God with authority, by the blood and in the name of Jesus Christ.

CHAPTER 6

JESUS' PIERCED FEET WON BACK DOMINION OVER THE PLACES WE WALK

The fifth place where Jesus shed His blood was where they drove the spikes through His feet, nailing Him to the cross. The blood shed from His feet also redeemed us from our loss of dominion and authority. Man was supposed to be the head and not the tail. Man was supposed to be above only and not beneath. (See Deuteronomy 28:13.) That is our place through the shed blood of Jesus. When Adam disobeyed God in the Garden of Eden, he lost our dominion and authority; and at that moment, Satan became the god of this world. But through Jesus' shed blood, we don't have to be trampled by Satan. Instead, we are to trample him!

> *Every place on which the sole of your foot treads shall be yours.* (Deuteronomy 11:24)

We have been commanded to *"go into all the world and preach the good news to all creation"* (Mark 16:15 NIV). Wherever we go, we're to tell people, *"The kingdom of God is near. Repent and believe the good news!"* (Mark 1:15 NIV). This would be impossible unless we had the authority to take dominion over Satan's earthly kingdom. We are told to *"be strong and courageous. Do not be afraid or terrified...for the* LORD *your God goes with you; he will never leave you nor forsake you"* (Deuteronomy 31:6 NIV). Dominion over this earth is ours again because of the shed blood of Jesus Christ, and wherever we are, the kingdom of heaven is at hand.

As a believer, you have the authority to walk around your neighborhood and say, "I bind the devil in my neighborhood. I bind the drug addicts and the dope dealers." You can walk through the schools and say, "I bind violence, I bind homosexuality, I bind perversion, and I bind New Age teaching," because wherever you go, God is with you.

The lawless and the gangs will yield to the power of God. You can stand on your front porch and say, "You spirit of violence, I bind you in the name of Jesus. I rebuke you out of my city. I command you to leave my neighborhood. I command you to leave my school. I command you to leave my government."

The enemy will say to you, "Who do you think you are?" And you can claim your position in God as His child, washed in the blood of Jesus with your dominion restored. Every place you put the soles of your feet, you are going to take dominion. God gives to you every place you lay the soles of your feet.

PLEADING THE BLOOD OVER YOUR FAMILY

At the beginning of this past school year, parents were expressing their concerns to me about the safety of their children during the school day. I told them what Moses told the children of Israel, "Put the blood of Jesus over your doorposts, because when that spirit of iniquity and destruction tries to come in, it will see the blood and flee." How do you put Jesus' blood on your doorpost? You speak the Word over your children. Believe His promises of protection for your family. Command the enemy to leave your children alone. Pray for your children, plead the blood of Jesus over them, and know that the angel of death and destruction cannot cross the blood. Go to the school when no one is there, lay hands on the front doors, and pray over that school. Walk around the school and claim it for the kingdom of God, because *"every place where you set your foot will be yours"* (Deuteronomy 11:24 NIV).

There are things in the natural you can do also. Be there for your children. Talk to them. Get to know their friends. Get involved in their school activities. Volunteer at their school. Be the parent who goes the extra mile. Make your children your passion.

The devil has been occupying our schools long enough. It is time to take back what the enemy has stolen and consecrate it for God's work. But don't stop there. Put the blood of Jesus over the tabernacle doors of your own life. Then, when that spirit of iniquity, death, and destruction comes, it understands that it cannot cross that blood line. It doesn't matter whether it is guns, divorce, poverty, or sickness, because *"He who is in you is greater than he who is in the world"* (1 John 4:4).

> *For the unbelieving husband has been sanctified through his wife, and the unbelieving wife has been sanctified through her believing husband. Otherwise your children*

would be unclean, but as it is, they are holy.
(1 Corinthians 7:14 NIV)

Your spouse may not be saved, but you can plead the blood over him or her and over your children and break that family curse. When we learned this years ago, we encouraged all the wives in our church who had unsaved husbands to start pleading the blood over their husbands. At first, the husbands were mad at their wives because they were going to church, but within two weeks, every one of those husbands came in and got saved. Thirty women were faithfully praying and thirty husbands gave their lives to Jesus. Why? Because the prayers of their wives broke the iniquity that was holding them in bondage. This will also work for your children. Through the power of the blood of Jesus, you can see your children turn their faces to God and live for Him. You can see your children rise up and make a godly impact on their schools. You can see your child stand against the wiles of the evil one and stand for righteousness.

When we were looking at a piece of property for the church, we went to the mayor, but the mayor said, "This is industrial, commercial property. No church can be allowed to be built here." That didn't stop us because we knew by the Spirit of God this was the land God had for us. We went out there, walked around that land, and claimed it for our church. Later, we met with the city council, who had already decided they were going to turn us down. They said, "We don't know why we're doing this, but we're going to 'grandfather' you in. You're the only church that's going to be able to build on this commercial property." God gave us dominion, and I knew that wherever I put the sole of my feet was blood-bought property.

We were originally planning to purchase fifty acres, but it ended up being eighty-four acres. Today, that land is worth more than five or six times the amount we paid for it. Not only does God give us dominion over the places we walk, He prospers the places we walk.

RISE UP AND TAKE DOMINION

But one testified in a certain place, saying: "What is man that You are mindful of him, or the son of man that You take care of him? You have made him a little lower than the angels; You have crowned him with glory and honor, and set him over the works of Your hands. You have put all things in subjection under his feet." For in that He put all in subjection under him, He left nothing that is not put under him. But now we do not yet see all things put under him.

(Hebrews 2:6–8)

We are not simply God's little boys and girls. You and I are heirs of salvation. That means that the angels are under us; we are not under them. We are joint heirs with Christ Jesus. (See Romans 8:17.) When we go where He tells us to go, He goes with us, and we are able to take dominion by His authority.

We don't serve a Savior who is dead or a Lord who is still in the tomb. We serve a resurrected Savior full of life, full of power, and full of anointing! Our burden-removing, yoke-destroying Savior says, "As My Father sent Me, now I am sending you. Wherever you go, tell them the kingdom of heaven is at hand." (See John 20:21 and Matthew 10:7.)

Years ago, people used to do "Jericho marches." Now, understand that there is no power in *religious ritual*, but there is life-changing power in *revelation*. The original Jericho march happened because Joshua received a revelation from the Lord that everywhere his feet trod would come under his God-given authority. (See Joshua 1:3.) Get concerned about your children's schools and walk around the school grounds and say, "Every place I put the soul of my feet is blood-bought ground for the kingdom of God. He gives it to us for an inheritance." Don't do this in a way that makes you look ridiculous, but you can march around that school, and the spirits of violence, anger, depression, and disease will crumble.

When the children of Israel put the blood of the lamb on their doorposts, the spirit of death could not cross. (See Exodus 12:22–28.) You need to put the blood around your house, your church, and your children's schools, and understand that God restored dominion to you by the blood that flowed from Jesus' feet.

When we bind the devil, our next step is to loose the peace of Jesus in our streets. Loose the righteousness of Jesus in our cities.

> *Truly I say to you, whatever you shall bind on earth shall be bound in heaven; and whatever you loose on earth shall be loosed in heaven.* (Matthew 18:18 NASB)

We can bind the enemy and kick him out of our cities and nation, but to keep him out, we must release the power of God to transform lives. We must preach the good news and make disciples of all people to really walk in dominion.

We say, "Well, God ought to do something about this mess."

He says, "I already did."

"God ought to send someone."

He says, "I'm trying! Are you listening?"

And he said unto them, Go ye into all the world, and preach the gospel to every creature....And these signs shall follow them that believe; in my name shall they cast out devils; they shall speak with new tongues; they shall take up serpents; and if they drink any deadly thing, it shall not hurt them; they shall lay hands on the sick, and they shall recover. (Mark 16:15, 17–18 KJV)

Are you ready to take dominion? Are you ready to take your town for Jesus? Are you ready to turn your nation back to God? It's time to go into the enemy's camp and take back what he has stolen!

DISCUSSION QUESTIONS

1. What does Deuteronomy 28:13 say the Lord will make you?

2. (a) According to Deuteronomy 11:24, what places will you have dominion over?

   Every place you put the soles of your feet

   (b) In Mark 16:15 (NIV), what are we commanded to do? *Preach the gospel*

   (c) Mark 1:15 says wherever we go, we are to tell people what? *Kingdom of God is at hand. repent + believe*

3. What are we told to be in Deuteronomy 31:6 (NIV)?

   Strong + Corageous

4. You can put the blood of Jesus over the tabernacle doors of your life because, according to 1 John 4:4:

   He who is in ___me___ is ___Greater___ than he who is in the world.

5. According to Romans 8:17, we are not simply God's little boys and girls. We are "___heirs___ of ___God___."

6. In Matthew 18:18, what does Jesus say to us about binding and loosing?

   What you bind on earth will be bound in heaven.

   Whatever you loose on earth shall be loosed in heaven.

CHAPTER 7

JESUS' PIERCED HEART WON BACK OUR JOY

*The Jews therefore, because it was the
preparation, that the bodies should not
remain upon the cross on the sabbath
day, (for that sabbath day was an high
day,) besought Pilate that their legs might
be broken, and that they might be taken
away. Then came the soldiers, and brake
the legs of the first, and of the other
which was crucified with him. But when
they came to Jesus, and saw that he was
dead already, they brake not his legs:
but one of the soldiers with a spear
pierced his side, and forthwith came
there out blood and water.*
—John 19:31–34 KJV

The sixth place Jesus shed His blood was where
a soldier shoved a spear into His side and blood
and water poured out. Jesus died so that we could
be forgiven. He was heartbroken from the weight of
our sins. We have all heard it said that the nails in
His hands and feet didn't hold Him on the cross;

His love for us did. As He hung on the cross, Jesus' heart broke for us. When the Roman soldier pierced His side, that blood from His broken heart flowed forth for us.

It was the rule of the observance of the Sabbath that there could not be anyone on the cross when the Sabbath began. Jesus was crucified on a Friday, and the Sabbath began at sunset that day. To comply with Jewish law, the soldiers went to each of the crucified to break their legs. This was to hasten their death so that they would be dead before the Sabbath began.

When someone died on the cross, he didn't die from the pain of the crucifixion in a few moments or an hour or so—it could take days. Eventually, he couldn't hold himself up any longer and the weight of his own body caused his lungs to collapse. He died a slow and horrible death from suffocation. However, according to the Jewish law, the body was not to remain on the cross overnight, so it was taken down and buried, lest the curse be transferred to the land. (See Deuteronomy 21:22–23.)

Scripture had prophesied that no bone in the Messiah's body would be broken. (See John 19:36 and Psalm 34:20.) When they got to Jesus to break His legs, they found there was no need, for He was already dead.

When Jesus announced His ministry in the synagogue, He read from the scroll:

The Spirit of the LORD is upon Me, because He has anointed Me to preach the gospel to the poor; He has sent Me to heal the broken-hearted, to proclaim liberty to the captives

and recovery of sight to the blind, to set at
liberty those who are oppressed.

(Luke 4:18)

Jesus was anointed with the burden-removing,
yoke-destroying power of God to heal the broken-
hearted. Why the brokenhearted? Because God desires for His people to live in joy. When we are filled
with joy, we have the strength to fight the good fight
of faith.

The joy of the LORD is your strength.

(Nehemiah 8:10)

Jesus will not only take your sin, but He'll also
take the pain of that sin. As the old saying goes,
"He'll turn our hurts into halos and our scars into
stars."

People do not despise a thief if he steals
to satisfy himself when he is starving. Yet
when he is found, he must restore seven-
fold; he may have to give up all the sub-
stance of his house. (Proverbs 6:30–31)

The devil is the one who comes to steal, kill,
and destroy. When you discover that we battle not
with flesh and blood, you'll realize that it's not people who steal life from you. The thief is not your ex-
wife, your ex-husband, or your ex-boss. The thief is
the devil. The Bible says so, and now he has to pay
you back sevenfold. Knowing that, you can say with
confidence, *"We know that all things work together*
for good to those who love God, to those who are the
called according to His purpose" (Romans 8:28).

Romans 8:28 is one of my favorite Scriptures in the Bible, because it is the only way we can carry out God's instruction to rejoice in the Lord always. You may say, "How can I rejoice after all I've been through?" Because God says that He can take even the worst things that happen to you and turn them to good. No matter what it is, the power of Jesus' blood will reverse it to your prosperity and your blessing.

Remember the story of Joseph? When he shared his dreams with his brothers, instead of rejoicing with him, they threw him into a pit and sold him into slavery. They told his father that he had died. Joseph went through incredible hardships, but eventually he ended up in the very place God had intended for him to be: the second most powerful man in all of Egypt. When famine hit the land, Joseph's brothers came to him for food. As he forgave his brothers and provided for them, Joseph gave us one of the greatest faith teachings in the Bible:

> *But as for you, you meant evil against me; but God meant it for good, in order to bring it about as it is this day, to save many people alive.* (Genesis 50:20)

Christians must get a revelation that what the devil means for evil in our lives, God will use it for our good. Why? Because Romans 8:28 says that all things work together for good for God's children, who love Him and are fulfilling His purpose in their lives. Now, that's something to give us joy!

The joy the enemy has stolen from you must be returned to you sevenfold. It's payday! Jesus said, "I've come to give you joy, I've come to give you life, and

I've come to give you good cheer." (See John 10:10.) Joy is to be the centerpiece of the Christian life. As a matter of fact, after we get saved and are baptized in the Holy Spirit, if we don't have joy, we have no strength. Jesus came to heal the brokenhearted, to restore our joy, and to renew our strength.

A woman in our church had suffered for over thirty years with bipolar disorder, also known as manic depression, an incurable genetic disease with a suicide rate of 20 percent because of the extreme depression it causes. She had been through everything medically possible, including psychiatric confinement and medication, to cure her wild and uncontrollable mood swings. Since she was ten years old, she suffered not only her own debilitating depression, but also the misunderstanding and rejection of people who didn't understand her extreme mood fluctuations. After we had prayed with her, this is what she wrote to us:

> Dear Pastor Huch,
>   Since being set free from generational curses, my moods are more stable than they have ever been in my whole life! My mental function is far beyond what I ever experienced or thought was possible. I'm claiming a sevenfold restoration in all areas that Satan has tried to destroy.
>
>   Shelly

For over two years now, she has been living a life of joy and freedom that she never thought possible. The joy of life is being restored to her because of the broken heart that Jesus suffered on the cross.

THE BROKEN HEART OF JESUS

Jesus knows what it is to suffer a broken heart, not just physically in His death on the cross but also through the betrayal and rejection by the very ones He came to love and call His friends. Many of those He ministered to cried, "Crucify Him!"

When Jesus stood before Pilate, the Roman governor in Israel, Pilate felt the conviction of the Holy Spirit. He wanted to release Jesus because he knew Jesus was without fault. Pilate's own wife even warned him, *"Have nothing to do with that just Man, for I have suffered many things today in a dream because of Him"* (Matthew 27:19). Pilate was looking for a way out, but he also wanted to please the people who were calling for Jesus' execution. In observance of the custom of Passover, a prisoner could be released, so Pilate suggested to the people that they choose Jesus.

> *Now at the feast he was accustomed to releasing one prisoner to them, whomever they requested. And there was one named Barabbas, who was chained with his fellow rebels; they had committed murder in the rebellion. Then the multitude, crying aloud, began to ask him to do just as he had always done for them. But Pilate answered them, saying, "Do you want me to release to you the King of the Jews?" For he knew that the chief priests had handed Him over because of envy. But the chief priests stirred up the crowd, so that he should rather release Barabbas to them. Pilate answered*

and said to them again, "What then do you want me to do with Him whom you call the King of the Jews?" So they cried out again, "Crucify Him!" Then Pilate said to them, "Why, what evil has He done?" But they cried out all the more, "Crucify Him!" So Pilate, wanting to gratify the crowd, released Barabbas to them; and he delivered Jesus, after he had scourged Him, to be crucified.
(Mark 15:6–15)

Jesus was the Son of God. He had the Spirit of God. But He was also flesh and blood, a man who felt the same way you and I feel. Jesus grew up in a family and lived and walked among people for thirty years. Then He walked among the people for three years of ministry. He loved people. He blessed people. Children ran up to Him and hugged Him. Then He was betrayed by Judas, one of the disciples whom He loved.

Jesus knew what it was to have a broken heart. First, one of His close friends betrayed Him and turned Him over to Roman authorities. Second, the very people He loved, the very people He ate with, healed, delivered, and blessed, began to cry out, "Give us the murderer Barabbas. Crucify Jesus." These very people whom He loved and who had walked with Him were striking Him, spitting on Him, mocking Him, and making a spectacle out of Him.

Then Peter denied Him three times. It would be like your best friend or your spouse looking at you and telling someone, "I don't know him or her." Jesus felt just like we would feel if that happened to us.

Jesus hung on the cross naked in front of His mother. They had ripped the beard from His face. They had put a cruel crown of thorns on His head to mock Him. Spit was running down His hair. On top of it all, every sin that had ever been committed—every lie, every murder, every rape, every pornographic picture, every drug addiction, every holocaust of terror—came on Him, the One who had never sinned. He took our sins upon Himself, and at that moment, God, His own Father, had no choice but to turn His back on Him.

> *And at the ninth hour Jesus cried out with a loud voice, saying, "Eloi, Eloi, lama sabachthani?" which is translated, "My God, My God, why have You forsaken Me?"*
> (Mark 15:34)

His heart was broken so your heart and my heart could be made whole. We overcome the wounds of broken hearts by the blood of the Lamb. Jesus became our sin so we wouldn't have to sin. He became our sickness so we wouldn't have to be sick. He became our broken heart so we wouldn't have to have a broken heart. Jesus came to restore our joy.

> *And God will wipe away every tear from their eyes; there shall be no more death, nor sorrow, nor crying. There shall be no more pain, for the former things have passed away.* (Revelation 21:4)

> *He heals the brokenhearted and binds up their wounds [curing their pains and their sorrows].* (Psalm 147:3 AMP)

GIVE GOD YOUR HURTS

If you don't allow God to heal your hurt, your untended hurt turns to bitterness. Jesus taught His disciples in Matthew 6:12 to pray, *"Forgive us our debts, as we forgive our debtors."* He then told them, *"If you forgive men when they sin against you, your heavenly Father will also forgive you. But if you do not forgive men their sins, your Father will not forgive your sins"* (Matthew 6:14–15 NIV).

This is how I learned how to forgive: I discovered who the thief is, and it isn't a person; it's the devil. I also realized that I battle not with flesh and blood. I refuse to battle with people; I battle with principalities and powers and rulers of darkness in high places. (See Ephesians 6:12.)

People are nothing more than tools of either God or the devil. If I lay my hands on a person and bless him, or I touch him and he's healed, who has blessed him? We know it is Jesus. But if I lay my hands on a person and destroy him or try to hurt what he's doing, who has hurt him? Most people will say that I did. However, I just chose to let the devil use me so that he could hurt someone. We've been trained to give God the *glory*, but we've got to be trained to give the devil the ultimate *blame*.

Now, don't misunderstand me. I'm not saying that people shouldn't be held accountable for their actions! If a man comes into my house and steals all I have, he must take responsibility for his actions. No court of law will excuse a crime because the criminal says, "The devil made me do it!" But as Christians, we must look beyond the person to the power behind his actions. And it also forces us to ask ourselves the question, "Just who is using me right now, Jesus or Satan?"

People are simply tools. If we're in the hands of the Carpenter, Jesus, we are used to build people up. If we're in the hands the destroyer, Satan, we are used to tear people down. Let me give you an example. A hammer is simply a tool. That hammer can build a wall or tear it down. If you see a wall, you don't give the hammer the glory. If you see a wall with holes punched in it, you don't blame the hammer. The hammer is just a tool in someone's hands. This is why Jesus said we battle not with flesh and blood but with evil spirits. Unfortunately, we've all been hammering on each other one minute and trying to build each other up the next.

In dealing with forgiveness, we must forgive in order to be forgiven, and in order to forgive, we must realize who the thief is. When we do, he has to return the joy of the Lord to us sevenfold. We must forgive those who hurt us, knowing that the one behind their actions against us is the devil.

> *Then Jesus said, "Father, forgive them, for they do not know what they do."*
> (Luke 23:34)

Jesus understood it was the devil, not the people, who was trying to destroy Him.

> *And they stoned Stephen as he was calling on God and saying, "Lord Jesus, receive my spirit." Then he knelt down and cried out with a loud voice, "Lord, do not charge them*

with this sin." And when he had said this,
he fell asleep.   (Acts 7:59–60)

Steven understood that our battle is not against flesh and blood.

Jesus will stop the curse and reverse its course. He will heal your pain, and once the healing has taken place, you won't be bitter anymore. Resentment and hatred will no longer be part of your life. Receiving the joy of the Lord will open the windows of heaven over your life.

- When you get your joy back, you become strong in faith.
- When you are set free, you're not bitter; you are better.
- When you are happy, your light shines to others who are hurting.

The Bible tells us to put our hands to the plow and not look back. We should not look at what could have been, what might have been. We must look forward! Our harvest of joy, blessing, and prosperity is not behind us but in front of us. The plow is the blood, and Jesus is the Lord of the harvest!

We received this letter from a woman who experienced brokenness and great sorrow stemming from the hardships of her young life. However, the Lord had more for her than she ever thought possible.

Dear Pastor Tiz,
*   I spent my teenage years in foster homes. I*
was lost and bitter, and for me, drugs and alcohol
were the "good life" I didn't have. Most of my adult

life I was a late-stage alcoholic and drug abuser. Due to fear and addictions, I was unable to work and lived on welfare for many years.

My alcoholism put me in situations where I was raped twice and beaten more times than I can count. It caused my children to be taken away from me. I lived in vileness, poverty, sickness, and sin. My life was utter despair and depravity.

In 1981, on my second round of treatment for chemical abuse, I managed to stay sober in Alcoholics Anonymous for one year. Then I became suicidal and wanted to end my life. I believed I was the worst sinner in the world and that God couldn't possibly love me.

One night, I was listening to a Christian album, and I surrendered my life to Jesus. My life has been radically changed since that time. I have now been sober for fifteen years due to the precious mercy and grace of my Savior.

When I had been sober for six years, I learned how to drive because I wanted to go to college. In 1993, I graduated from Portland State University with high honors and was accepted to medical school on a state grant. I am on the Dean's List at my medical school and was nominated for "Who's Who among Students in Universities and Colleges in America" for 1996. All to the glory of God.

I believe the Lord has brought me to New Beginnings for a divine purpose. I praise God for all you and your staff are doing for those who lived as I had and for others who are lost and helpless.

I thank God every day for what He has done. What would I have done without my Savior? Jesus is truly "able to do exceedingly abundantly above all that we ask or think" *(Ephesians 3:20).*

Nicole

Healing broken hearts is not something we can do ourselves; it is something God has already done. We must claim it. Even if you have walked for years with a broken heart, Jesus Christ will make you every bit whole. Today, allow the healing power of Jesus Christ to deliver you from all pain, sorrow, and grief. Let Him fill you with the joy of the Lord, and let that joy become your strength, not just for today, but for the rest of your life.

The LORD's lovingkindnesses indeed never cease, for His compassions never fail. They are new every morning; great is Thy faithfulness. (Lamentations 3:22–23 NASB)

DISCUSSION QUESTIONS

1. (a) According to Jewish law, why was a body not to remain on the cross overnight? See Deuteronomy 21:22–23. *It cursed the land*

   (b) Scripture had prophesied that no bone in the Messiah's body would be broken. When the soldiers got to Jesus to break His legs, what did they discover? See John 19:36 and Psalm 34:20. *He was already dead*

2. What did Jesus say He came to do? Read Luke 4:18 and list the things the Spirit anointed Him to do. *heal the broken hearted, liberty to the captives, sight to the blind*

3. What does Proverbs 6:30–31 say the devil must restore to you? *sevenfold*

4. It is not people who steal life from you. The thief is the devil, and now he has to pay you back sevenfold. Knowing this, what can you say with confidence, according to Romans 8:28?

5. As Joseph forgave his brothers and provided for them, what great faith teaching did he give us in Genesis 50:20?

In order to save many people

6. Jesus knew what it was to have a broken heart. Read each of the following Scriptures, and list the heartbreaking circumstances surrounding His death:

(a) Mark 14:10–11

(b) Mark 14:72

(c) Mark 15:11–14

7. What did Jesus cry out in Mark 15:34?

8. Jesus' heart was broken so your heart could be made whole. How does Psalm 147:3 prove this statement?

9. What did Jesus teach His disciples to pray in Matthew 6:12, 14–15?

10. We must forgive those who hurt us, knowing that the one behind their actions against us is the devil. What did Jesus say in Luke 23:34 that demonstrates this principle?

CHAPTER 8

JESUS' BRUISES WON OUR DELIVERANCE FROM INNER HURTS AND INIQUITIES

But He was wounded for our transgres-
sions, He was bruised for our iniquities;
the chastisement for our peace was upon
Him, and by His stripes we are healed.
—Isaiah 53:5

The seventh place Jesus shed His blood was in His bruises. He went to the gates of hell and took back the keys to the kingdom to break every curse of iniquity. Not only was He wounded for our transgressions; this verse says, "He was bruised for our iniquities." As we discussed before, *iniquity* means "a wicked act or sin," but the Holy Spirit has shown me that *iniquity* can also be understood as any spirit that tries to break us down. It is a spiritual force on the inside that pressures us to bow or bend under its destructive nature.

If you have a bruise on your body, it means you are bleeding on the *inside*. Some bruises last a long time and go very deep. God said, "Not only will I forgive what you've done on the *outside*, but I'm going to give you power on the *inside* so you can walk in total victory."

CHANGED FROM THE INSIDE OUT

The Bible says that the iniquities of the father are passed down to the third and fourth generation— from the father to the children and to their children's children. The iniquity may be something *in* your family or *on* your family. But it is a driving demonic force within a person that causes that person harm in some way. Jesus said, "Not only was I wounded to forgive you for your sins, but I was also bruised on the inside to do a miracle within you, allowing you to go from an angry man to a godly man. You'll go from an addicted child to a child who is set free. You'll go from a woman who was suicidal to a woman full of joy because My blood is greater than any demonic force that comes against you."

When I talk about breaking a generational curse, I am not talking about struggling against a character weakness or family curse for the rest of your life. I am talking about being redeemed by the blood of Jesus. I am talking about being healed physically, emotionally, and spiritually. We can plead the blood of Jesus to wipe away our sin and to set us free from the iniquity that drives us to do the very thing we do not want to do.

> *And He died for all, that those who live should live no longer for themselves, but for Him who died for them and rose again.... Therefore, if anyone is in Christ, he is a new creation; old things have passed away;*

behold, all things have become new.
(2 Corinthians 5:15, 17)

When someone has suffered a physical strike or a blow, they develop a discolored bruise. Yet a person who has been bruised on the inside often doesn't show that hurt on the outside. We go around to one another saying, "How are you doing?" We reply, "Great, man!" but on the inside we are saying to ourselves, "Horrible." We say on the outside that things are tremendous, but on the inside we are saying, "I'm dying."

A woman might be sitting in the pew singing "What a Mighty God We Serve" and clapping her hands with everyone else around her, but inside she's grieving. She feels lonely and doesn't know how to have friends. She was molested as a child, and she is bruised. When a part of our body gets bruised, that area becomes tender, and we don't want anyone touching it. It hurts too much!

Our bruises don't always show. We put on a good face and cover it up well because we are people of faith and we believe we are to rejoice in the Lord always. However, on the inside, we are desperately hurting. We have been knocked down, ground down, and beaten down, and we think that because we are "overcoming" Christians, we are never to let anyone know about this.

A member at New Beginnings Christian Center shared her testimony of God healing her on the inside.

Dear Pastor Huch,
I am an ex-drug addict and an ex-prostitute.
I am one of those people no one wanted. I attended

church until the age of five. I never forgot about God, even though for most of my life I did not live for Him.

When I first got born again, I started attending New Beginnings Church. I believe Pastor Huch and I believe in his ministry. I am happy to be in the church and I am so happy to be alive and serving God.

Laura

We prayed for Laura, and God broke the curses of poverty, addictions, and low self-esteem that were on her life. She earned her GED, went to college, got a good job, and became one of the greatest givers in the church. She is also a regular soulwinner and a mentor to young girls coming off the streets.

When someone is bruised, it means he is bleeding not on the outside but on the inside. God said, "Not only will I forgive what he's done on the outside, but I'm going to change that person on the inside." Jesus shed His blood on the inside as well as on the outside. He was bruised inside to change the person on the inside, to change the nature that causes him hurt or suffering. Through His shed blood, we are not just free; we are free indeed!

For He made Him who knew no sin to be sin for us, that we might become the righteousness of God in Him. (2 Corinthians 5:21)

DISCUSSION QUESTIONS

1. Read Isaiah 53:5 and fill in the blanks below.

   But He was _____ for our _____, He was _____ for our _____; the chastisement of our peace was upon Him, and by His _____ we are healed.

2. Larry writes,

   When I talk about breaking a generational curse, I am not talking about struggling against a character weakness or family curse for the rest of your life. I am talking about being redeemed by the blood of Jesus. I am talking about being healed physically, emotionally, and spiritually. We can plead the blood of Jesus to wipe away our sin and to set us free from the iniquity that drives us to do the very thing we do not want to do. The key to receiving the blessing of God is not just getting saved, but getting changed—transferred from the old creature to the new!

   How does 2 Corinthians 5:15, 17 support his comment?

3. What assurance did Jesus give us in John 8:30 that through His shed blood we are free?

ENDNOTES

[1] Strong, "Greek Dictionary of the New Testament," #4982.

[2] Ibid., #3528.

[3] Strong, "Hebrew and Chaldee Dictionary," #3084.

[4] T. Rees, "God," *New International Bible Encyclopedia*, vol. II (Grand Rapids, MI: Wm. B. Eerdmans Publishing Co., 1956, reprinted 1980), 1254.

[5] Strong, "Hebrew and Chaldee Dictionary," #2250 and "Greek Dictionary of the New Testament," #3468.

[6] Strong, "Hebrew and Chaldee Dictionary," #693.

ABOUT THE AUTHOR

Larry Huch is the founder and senior pastor of DFW New Beginnings in Irving, Texas. Founded in November 2004, this nondenominational church has quickly developed into a diverse, multiethnic congregation of several thousand people. Pastor Larry and his wife, Tiz, are driven by a passionate commitment to see people succeed in every area of life. That passion, along with their enthusiasm, genuine love for people, and effective teaching, has fueled a ministry that spans over thirty years and two continents.

That same energy and commitment to sharing a positive, life-changing, and biblically based message with the world is the hallmark of Pastor Larry's international television program, *New Beginnings*. This program is broadcast weekly to millions of homes around the globe and has served to touch and change the lives of countless people.

Pastor Larry's signature combination of humor, a dynamic teaching style, and a deep understanding of the Bible have made him a much sought after guest on television programs, conferences, and various other forms of media. Pastor Larry is a pioneer in the area of breaking family curses and has been recognized the world over for his teachings on the subject, along with his best-selling book *Free at Last*. His successful follow-up book, *10 Curses That Block the Blessing*, is also a best seller. As a successful author, Pastor Larry has been honored by the testimonies of thousands of people whose lives have been impacted and forever altered by his testimony and teachings.

Pastor Larry is wholeheartedly committed to bridging the gap between Christians and Jews and restoring the church to its Judeo-Christian roots, which motivated him to write his latest books, *The Torah Blessing* and *Unveiling Ancient Biblical Secrets*. He firmly believes in studying, understanding, and teaching the Word from a Jewish perspective. Larry was honored to have spoken at the Israeli Knesset and has received awards from the Knesset Social Welfare Lobby for his ministry's generosity toward the needs of the Jewish people in Israel.

Pastors Larry and Tiz are the proud parents of three wonderful children (and a son-in-law and daughter-in-law), all of whom are active in ministry. Their grandchildren, their "Sugars," are the loves of their lives!

For more information
on Pastor Larry Huch's ministry,
visit his Web site:
www.larryhuchministries.com